Lost Homes

The Untold Stories

Inspiring Stories of Survival, Resilience, and Hope

Prodipta Soni

ISBN

Hardcase 979-8-89446-209-7
Paperback 979-8-89446-208-0

Disclaimer

The book *Lost Homes: The Untold Stories* is inspired by true-life incidents. While the plots are based in part on real events, the characters and the names of organizations mentioned in this book are entirely fictitious. Any resemblance to actual persons, living or dead, or to actual organizations, is purely coincidental.

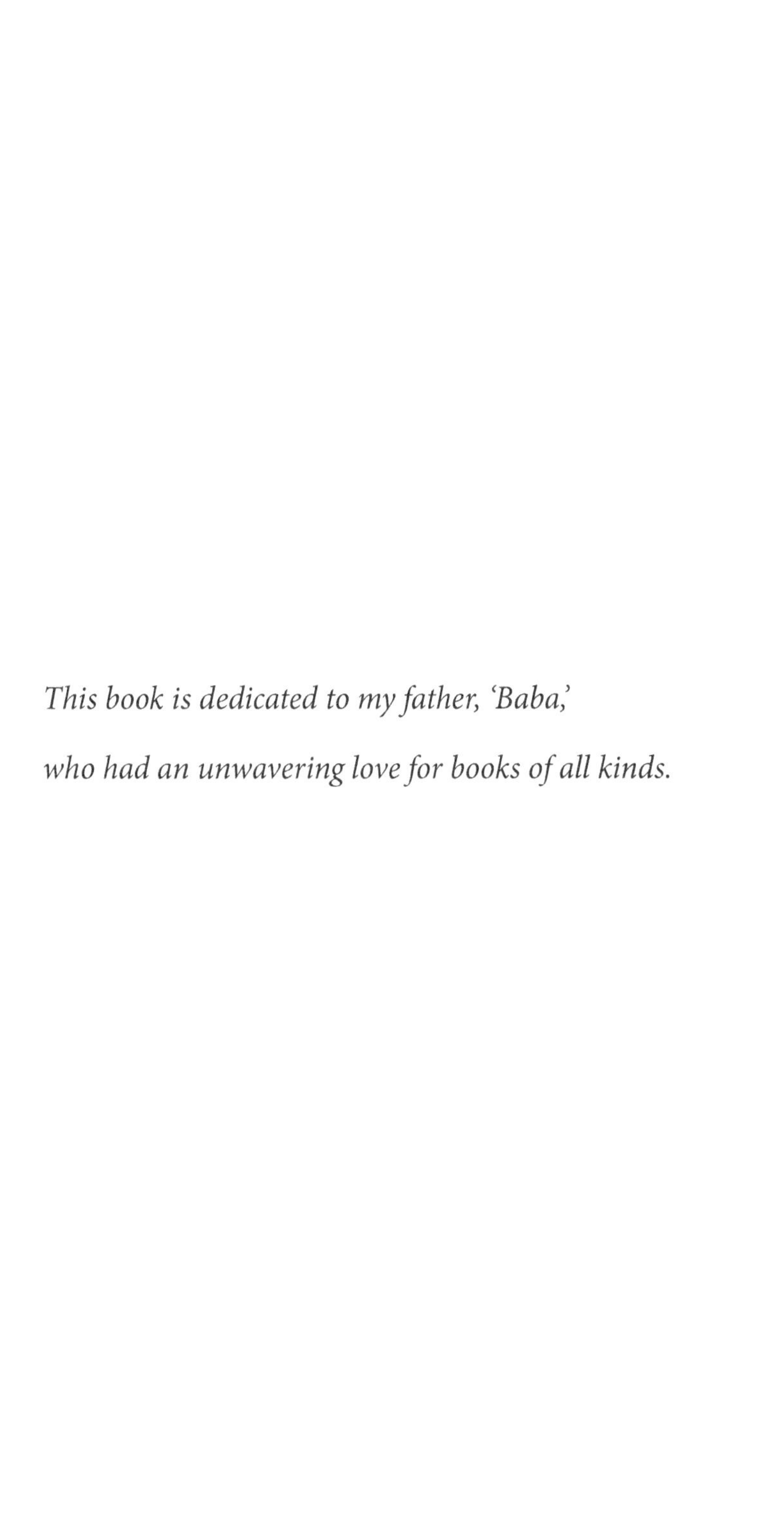

This book is dedicated to my father, 'Baba,'

who had an unwavering love for books of all kinds.

Contents

Foreword

*L*ost Homes is a book inspired by real-life stories of the extreme hardships faced by many of the world's children. Orphaned due to wars, disease, migrations, and other circumstances, these children must come to terms with their reality and chart their own path. Despite their hardships, there is always light and hope for a better life, often coming in the form of a caring aid worker, volunteer, or orphanage. Beyond the news bites and statistics of the many tragedies we read about, this book uncovers the harsh realities of orphaned children across the world. It is a must-read for everyone, helping us to empathize with individuals living through these devastating events and encouraging us to do our part to make the world safer for all children.

– Mohini Venkatesh,
Advisor, Save the Children Federation.

Introduction

This book is the culmination of inspiration drawn from a real-life incident that occurred three years ago, igniting a creative journey to delve into the depths of human experiences and emotions. It was November 14th, Children's Day, a day that remains etched in my memory. I was dealing with a personal issue that had left me feeling deeply sad, and I thought, "What better way to overcome my sadness than by bringing some joy to someone's life?" With this in mind, I decided to visit a nearby orphanage for the first time.

As I entered the orphanage, the lady in charge welcomed me warmly and guided me to the first floor where all the children had gathered in a large room. Almost all of them were below six years of age, except for one girl, Rupa (name changed to protect identity), who sat quietly in a corner. I remember vividly the first time I saw her: a quiet girl of about twelve years old with bright, big eyes, squatting on the floor. Rupa had cerebral palsy, which made it impossible for her to stand or walk. The only way she could communicate was through her smiles. In another corner of the room, I was surprised to see a boy of about seven or eight years old chained to a bed. He was extremely restless, his head constantly shaking as if he were trying to convey something. When I asked the lady in charge why he was restrained, she explained that he becomes aggressive, hitting both others and himself. The sight of him in such a state deeply saddened me, and even now, I regret that I could do nothing to help him on that day.

Later, I was completely taken aback by the shocking backgrounds of some of the children. True horrific incidents, such as a child witnessing the murder of one parent by the other and being left alone in the room with the corpse for hours before being rescued, shook me to the core.

Despite the circumstances, the children's innocence was heartwarming, and their boundless enthusiasm to learn new things was overwhelming. I just could not imagine the little children surviving in this world without the love and security of their parents. One by one, the children came near me to touch my fingers with theirs, each child doing the same thing. We sang Bollywood songs together, and some of the kids danced, filling the room with joy and laughter.

That night and the subsequent nights later, I could not sleep thinking about Sunil and Rupa. The memory stayed tucked away in a safe corner of my mind. That visit changed my life. It made me think of the thousands of innocent children across the world who endure unimaginable hardships, yet still find the strength to smile each day and hope for a better future. The resilience and quiet courage of these children humbled me, inspiring a profound sense of responsibility to make a difference in their lives.

Months later, when I made up my mind to write about children who live challenging lives, the first children who came to my mind were these abandoned children who lost their homes forever—hence Lost Homes.

Each narrative in this book explores the lives of such children across different cultures and countries, showing how, in the face of tragedy, the human spirit can not only endure but flourish. The last story in this book (Beat Of A Heart) is particularly close to my heart and home. It is based on the firsthand account of a child who stayed in an orphanage near my home in the suburbs of Mumbai. I met her several times. I set this story in Kolkata, my birthplace.

Through this book, I aim to uncover the untold stories of abandoned children across the world, hoping to inspire empathy and action in everyone who reads it. By understanding their lives, we can all do our part to make the world a safer, kinder place for all children.

– Prodipta Soni
Pune

If I can stop one heart from breaking,

I shall not live in vain;

If I can ease one life the aching,

Or cool one pain,

Or help one fainting robin

Unto his nest again, I shall not live in vain.

– Emily Dickinson

A Home Away From Home

Under the brilliant midday sun, its warmth contrasting with the chilling grip of the Himalayas, a weary group of children and a man cross the snowy landscape. Despite the strong sun, a biting cold seeps under their skin. The harsh journey makes them pant, their heavy breathing forming puffs of visible warmth in the crisp mountain air. For seven gruelling days, the children walk on the icy terrain of the world's highest mountains, each step a battle against chilling winds and biting cold. Everywhere their eyes wander, a vast expanse of white stretches out, devoid of any hint of life or greenery.

One boy, Tenzin, cannot walk anymore, his feet aching for the past two days. They have swollen up and burn like fire. Tenzin cries and wants to turn back, but it is impossible. Tenzin and the other five children are being led by a man who is helping them reach India from Tibet via Nepal illegally. Other than the six-year-old Tenzin, in this group are little Pema, a mere three-year-old, eight-year-old Dorje, nine-year-old Sonam, and twelve-year-old Jigme.

Ten Days Earlier

Amidst the majestic peaks of Tibet, where prayer flags whisper in the mountain breeze, the air is crisp with the scent of juniper and pine. The sun casts a golden hue upon the snow-capped summits. Here, Tibetan spirituality prevails throughout the entire region, with ancient monasteries clinging to the mountainsides, creating a picture of peace and quiet.

Norbu and Dawa are seated on handcrafted wooden stools outside their home in the Tibetan village of Gyantse. Their youngest son, Tenzin, and his sister play amidst a patch of wildflowers nearby. Their house, constructed from locally sourced stone and timber, emits a rustic charm that blends with the surroundings. The entrance to the house is marked by a simple wooden door, weathered by years of exposure. Above the door, a string of prayer flags flutter at the slightest hint of wind. A traditional wood-burning stove, its chimney reaching towards the sky, stands as the heart of the home, providing both warmth and nourishment to the family. In one corner, a small shrine adorned with flickering butter lamps and fragrant juniper incense pays homage to the family's Buddhist beliefs.

On this day, the parents wear a pensive look. They have just made the most crucial and painful choice of their lives. Tenzin, their oldest son, will be sent to Dharamshala, India, to attend the Dalai Lama school. However, sending him there means it's unlikely they will see their son again in this lifetime. Raising children in Tibet's repressive political environment, where their traditional way of life is being threatened, is a challenging task. For this reason, common Tibetans like Norbu and Dawa, who still value their spiritual and cultural legacy, have their children transported across the Chinese border into the care of the Dalai Lama and his government-in-exile, even though the journey puts their lives in danger.

A few days later, Tenzin stands with his father in Lhasa's town center, gripping his hand tightly. The air is filled with the chatter of locals and the occasional rumble of vehicles. Tenzin observes some Buddhist monks in their maroon robes as they quietly move through the streets of Lhasa. The smell of yak meat and freshly steamed momos wafts through the air, reminding Tenzin of his mother's cooking. A gentle evening breeze brushes against Tenzin's face and stirs memories of his village home.

Suddenly, Tenzin sees a tall, magnificent building in red and white towering over the city. "Apa! Look at that massive building over there! It's huge!"

"Yes, Tenzin. That's the Potala Palace, the most magnificent and important building in all of Tibet," said his father, smiling at Tenzin.

Tenzin exclaims, his excitement momentarily overpowering his worry and anxiety, "The Potala Palace? The one you've mentioned to me before?"

"That's right, son. Remember how I've described it to you, with its towering red and white walls, overlooking the city?" his father remarks, pleased to be able to offer this incredible sight to his son as a parting gesture, a cherished desire he had longed to fulfill.

In Lhasa, the Potala signifies Tibet's rich legacy. Its neighbouring government buildings and commercial complexes, designed in modern Chinese architectural styles with glass facades and clean lines, stand in stark contrast to traditional Tibetan architecture. Chinese security forces keep a noticeable presence in the city, closely examining everyone through surveillance cameras and checkpoints.

Tenzin and his father are to meet a man here in Lhasa who will take Tenzin and some other children safely to India. They are to flee secretly in the middle of the night.

Fear and uncertainty cloud Tenzin's thoughts. He tries to recall his mother's assurance of safety and education in India, but all he wants is to stay in the moment, feeling the comfort of his father by his side, knowing he will soon be on his own. He holds tightly to his father's hand, scared of the Chinese policemen who are checking everyone's passports. Their stern faces and rigid postures instill a sense of unease amongst the passersby, especially those awaiting inspection. None of them have any papers and their hearts pound in silent apprehension.

Tenzin and his father wait for a few hours until it grows dark. At a pre-designated spot in town, they meet a man and some other children. The man leads them to a dark alley where a truck stands waiting, barely visible in the shadows. The alley is dark and musty and reeks of petrol.

"Go ba kyop pa!" says the man in Tibetan.

The children hurriedly climb into the truck. Inside, it is dark and stuffy. They sit on the floor of the truck, anxious, and talk in hushed tones. Tenzin, with his innocent eyes, observes the varying reactions around him. His eyes fall upon a little girl huddled in one corner. He smiles at her but her face shows no expression. As the last child climbs aboard, the man slams the door shut, cutting them off from the familiar world. Tenzin wants to run to his mother. He closes his eyes and says a little prayer his grandmother had taught him. The air is suffocating, the darkness pressing in on him like a heavy blanket. As the truck starts moving, faint beams of light filter through some holes in the sides. Tenzin, perched on the edge of his seat, strains to catch a glimpse of the world outside, but he cannot see anything. The road is bumpy, and Tenzin's head keeps hitting the truck walls. He tries to protect himself with his hands but still gets hurt. Every time he bangs his head, he cries. The children sit in silence, too tired to speak. Eventually, they drift off to sleep.

A few hours later, they are woken up by a voice shouting, "Get down quickly, I don't want the Chinese guards to see us!"

Tenzin awakes to the glaring sunlight coming through the half-open door of the truck, his eyes stinging from the sudden glare of light. Their guide is standing outside the door. As the children step out, all they can see is a desolate, snowy landscape stretching endlessly before them. Their guide tells them that they have reached the Tibetan border. The cold bites into their skin, and the sound of their footsteps crunching the snow makes them feel increasingly uneasy. Tenzin wraps his jacket tighter around himself. In Tibet, they wear thick, insulated robes called chubas, but today, for the Himalayan journey, they all wear thick insulated jackets along with sturdy boots, hats, and gloves made from yak wool.

Tenzin notices the youngest girl shivering uncontrollably despite her warm clothing. Without hesitation, the guide drapes a larger coat around her, offering what little warmth he can. As the truck departs, leaving them alone in the frigid landscape, the children huddle closer, speaking in hushed tones.

"Come on, get moving, or we shall be stuck in this snow-land forever." In the clear light of day, the children finally take a good look at their guide and notice that he is a well-built Tibetan man. His face is rough and bears marks of years spent in extreme conditions. Yet something about him suggests that beneath his rough exterior, he has a kind heart.

Present Day

The guide looks at Tenzin's black-speckled feet and says that he has frostbite. The other children cast anxious glances at each other, too cold to speak. The fight against fatigue and the haunting fear of leaving their parents behind has worn them down, bit by bit. The group presses on, driven by a desperate determination to reach India, where they hope to find safety and a chance at a better life. They walk through thick blankets of snow until they reach a place called Sha-Go-La, near the Tibet-Nepal border.

As they ascend higher into the mountains, the weather changes abruptly. Dark clouds gather overhead, and the air becomes thick. The guide, with his years of experience sensing the weather at these high altitudes, urges the children to move faster, understanding that a snowstorm approaches. The wind picks up, carrying icy particles that sting the children's faces. The temperature drops even more, and soon, snow starts falling, gently at first but gradually turning into heavy, swirling blankets, a full-fledged Himalayan snowstorm.

The biting cold intensifies, and the visibility diminishes rapidly. The children, already fatigued and disheartened, struggle to keep up. Tenzin, with his frostbitten feet, moves with agonizing slowness. The guide shouts above the howling wind, instructing the children to seek refuge beneath a cluster of rocks. The ground is covered in layers of snow, and although they try clearing it, it is impossible with the icy winds. All the food gets buried in the snow. They nestle together beneath the rocks for the night.

By the next morning, the snowstorm had subsided. When the group resumes their laborious trek, snow reaches to their chest. Pema has to be carried by the guide.

After walking for two more days, the children begin to faint and struggle hard to continue without food. 8-year-old Dorje and 9-year-old Sonam succumb to the harsh conditions, dying within 30 minutes of each other. While their parents carry on with their lives in Tibet, the beat of their hearts must have faltered the moment their children drew their last breath in snowy graves. They know not their dreams of their children learning about their nation's rich history lay shattered. These young children sacrifice their lives for the sake of their homeland. The guide, facing the grim reality, has to leave their lifeless bodies in the snow, their heads turned towards India and the distant hope embodied by His Holiness the Dalai Lama.

As the freezing wind cuts through their clothing, only Jigme, Tenzin and Pema manage to survive. Jigme, still reasonably healthy and older, carries little Pema on his back. Tenzin's feet are making it impossible for him to walk. Jigme has put tsampa (roasted barley flour) in his shoes, rationing it in small bits for survival. Their guide informs them that they still have eight more days of travel ahead. The children nod, too tired to speak.

After eight days, they reach the Nepalese military checkpoint. To make it past this hurdle, they must carry on at night. The guide, wary of detection, herds them close together, whispering, "No lights. We must stay invisible."

Under the cover of darkness, the group moves silently, relying on the moonlight to guide them. Finally, after a grueling 14-hour march through cold and snow, they reach a Sherpa's hut. Completely exhausted, they knock at the door. The kind Sherpa understands the urgency of their situation and says, "Please, come in."

He welcomes them with a warm hearth—the first they have seen since leaving Tibet. Inside the Sherpa's low-ceilinged hut, a stove burns at the center with a large pot atop it. Their frozen and starved bodies start to warm up from the heat, like a gentle hug thawing their chilled limbs.

"You must be hungry. Sit, sit."

The children, their faces gaunt and weary, settle around a low table. The Sherpa's wife brings out steaming bowls of noodles made with vegetables and meat. "Eat," the Sherpa says, handing out chopsticks. "You need your strength." They eat quickly and quietly.

Tenzin looks at Pema, who manages a small smile. Over dinner, the guide speaks with the Sherpa, his voice low and earnest. "These children... I want to give them a chance to study, to meet His Holiness the Dalai Lama."

The Sherpa nods. "You are doing a noble thing. They will be safe here tonight. Rest well."

That night, as they settle in to sleep, Pema begins to cry, her small body trembling. "I miss Mama," she whispers, her voice choked with tears.

The guide kneels beside her, wrapping a comforting arm around her shoulders. "I know, little one. Your mother would be proud of your bravery. We're almost there. Just a little longer."

Pema nods, her tears subsiding. She soon falls asleep.

The next morning, they set off again. It takes them a few more days to reach the Namoche Gyasa Reception Centre for Tibetan refugees in Nepal. Here they get a refugee pass, which allows them to continue their journey to Dharamshala in Northern India. Tenzin has to have his toes amputated in a hospital in Nepal, while the guide is treated for severe frostbite. Only Jigme and three-year-old Pema are not affected as badly.

A few days later, Jigme, Tenzin and Pema arrive in Dharamshala just as the sun rises over the mountains. Their guide leaves for Tibet to bring another set of children to India. Before leaving, he takes a group photo to show to the parents of the children that their loved ones made it safely into Indian exile.

Jigme, Tenzin and Pema have been through one of the toughest ordeals of their lives. They have crossed the forbidden frontier and left their own country behind, lost to them forever. The land on which they now stand will be theirs for years to come, becoming their home away from home.

In recent years, approximately 50 to 60 Tibetan children per year have fled Tibet and made the perilous journey across the Himalayas to seek refuge in India. This number has decreased from earlier decades due to increased border security and the dangers associated with the journey. Many of these children aim to receive education in Tibetan schools in exile and connect with their cultural heritage under the guidance of the Tibetan Government-in-Exile in Dharamshala.

In Another World

Part 1

Ahmed

In war-torn Gaza, even as missiles were being dropped in several regions, it is a busy morning on a corner street as people go about buying their daily supplies of food and groceries. Little Ahmed is nervous on his way to the market. His mother is sick this morning and she also has to look after his younger brothers, so she has sent Ahmed for milk and bread. It has been days since a nearby area was heavily bombarded, and many shops have been closed indefinitely.

The air feels dense, distant explosions contributing to an overarching sense of foreboding. As Ahmed moves through the market, he notices that the meat shop, usually packed with people waiting in line, is now vacant. The absence of hanging meat makes the place feel strangely empty. Close by, the vegetable shop next to it has only a few baskets of dried vegetables. A small group of men is trying to lay claim on whatever they can.

Walking down the market road, Ahmed's eyes fix upon the sweet shop, a place filled with happy memories of visits with his father. Mutabak is a family favourite treat—a delectable pie dough soaked in sweet syrup and sugar. He remembers the first time he tasted it, the memory making him salivate. But today, the shop, though open, presents a grim picture. The glass displays, once adorned with Gaza's famous sweets, stand bare. Ahmed hurries past until he reaches the only milk shop which is open, joining a small queue.

The faces of those around him bear vacant expressions. Ahmed wonders if he is the only one feeling terrified. Puzzled by why, in the face of imminent danger, people persist in their everyday tasks, he simply longs to go home and be with his mother and brothers. His hands tremble as he quickly tucks the packet of milk into a cloth bag that his mother gave him hesitantly that morning.

It is the first time she has sent her little boy to the market. While she is certain he will be able to find his way, as he has been to the market many times with his father, her heart still worries. Tears well in her eyes as she reminisces about the countless occasions she gave that same bag to her husband until a few weeks ago when he lost his life in an airstrike while away for work. His body was never recovered.

As the sound of explosions draws nearer and people start panicking, Ahmed quickly searches for the shop that sells bread but cannot locate it in the confusion. He sees people hurrying back and quickly follows their cue to head home. Soon people start running frantically in every direction. Clutching the cloth bag to his chest, Ahmed walks as fast as his little feet could take him. When he reaches his home, his heart sinks.

Where his house had been, where his family lived there was nothing but a big heap of rubble. His little brothers, who used to laugh and play around the house, are nowhere to be found. Even his mother he cannot see anywhere. Unable to take in what has happened, Ahmed starts crying. The war has taken away his family.

After a while, as Ahmed looks at the ruins of what was once his home, he spots a tattered photo album lying in the debris. With trembling hands, he flips through the pages, blackened and stained with soot. Most of the photographs are barely recognizable, but one image remains intact—a snapshot of his father beaming proudly alongside Ahmed and his brothers. Fresh tears blur Ahmed's vision as he clutches the photograph to his chest. Amongst the familiar faces, Ahmed's eyes settle on his own face, the only one still discernible despite the soot and dust.

A few hours later, rescue personnel take him to safety.

Amal

As airstrikes continue in some parts of Gaza, one can see buildings razed to nothing more than piles of rubble, with families camped out on the small mountains of busted concrete and mangled steel that were once their homes. Situated in a neighbourhood within Gaza, Amal's home is part of a handful that has not yet faced the devastating impact of bombardment. The area, though bearing the atmosphere of impending danger, retains traces of its former life.

The narrow streets, once filled with the laughter of children and the chatter of neighbours, now carry an uneasy quiet. In one such home, a family of three has gathered around their small breakfast table. Amal stares at her half-eaten breakfast, her face pale, worry evident in her furrowed brows. Amal's father notices her silence and gently asks, "What's on your mind, Amal?"

"Baba, will we never need to go to school again and study?"

Her father responds, "Why do you say that, Amal?"

In a voice filled with concern, Amal answers, "Because, Baba, we'll only be killed soon. What's the point of going to school if we are all going to die?"

Her parents exchange glances and stay silent for a while. Finally, Amal's father speaks in a low voice, "We'll find a safer place soon, alright?"

Amal's mother, her eyes reflecting the weariness of living in a conflict zone, looks at her husband with a mix of concern and uncertainty. "Safer place? How can we be sure, Habib? Is there any safe place in Gaza anymore?" She sounds tired and unsure.

Just as the words hang in the air, the sound of missiles interrupts their conversation. The family leaves their breakfast in a hurry, rushing to the window. Amal's mother freezes in fear. The moment they have been fearing for months has arrived at last.

Amal's father urgently instructs, "Everyone, stay away from the windows! Get low, quickly!"

In the midst of the chaos, two missiles hit their home, shaking everything. The explosions are deafening. One falls on Amal's mother, shattering her into pieces, and the other rips through her father.

Amal struggles to stand in the home that is no more, shocked by what surrounds her. Suddenly, despite the piercing sounds of bombardment, she feels enveloped by silence. The only sound that stands out is the deafening wail of ambulance sirens. She covers her ears in anguish and whispers, looking at the devastated bodies of her parents who were alive just a few moments ago, "We'll get through this. Help is on the way."

Hana

Hana begs her parents, "Mom, Dad, take Rami and go! I'll wait for the rescue team. I'll be okay," uncertainty filling her voice as she sits in her wheelchair.

Hana's mother insists, "We can't leave you alone. It's too dangerous."

When the military warned everyone in the north of Gaza to evacuate south before an airstrike near their home, authorities alerted the same to the 50 people in the residential building where Hana stayed with her family.

The urgently broadcasted evacuation orders unleashed utter panic within the five-story structure. The residents fled the building and migrated to a nearby hospital, everyone except for Hana and her family. Nine-year-old Hana has been in a wheelchair all her life.

"We stay together as a family. We'll be okay," says Hana's father. The impending danger outside intensifies as the military warnings blare the same evacuation message over and over again.

As the clock ticks on, Hana's parents still hope for the rescue team to arrive in time, their hearts weighing down. The far-off sound of an approaching aircraft grows into a loud roar, muffling the alarmed cries of the city. In an instant, the building shudders, debris rains down, and a plume of dust engulfs everything.

Hana and her family are thrust into a dark world of choking dust, smoke, and fire. Everything seems to vanish all at once. Hana can only feel the pain coursing through her body, trapped under the weight of the ceiling crushing her and her family.

In a panic, she screams the names of her parents and her little brother one by one. Unable to see or hear any of them, she prays and cries that one of them would answer her. None of them do. Soon, she passes out.

Hours later, it's the voices that come first. Muffled shouts of "She's alive!" become, "She's breathing!" It doesn't matter to her. All she cares about is whether her family is safe.

"Things will be okay," a stranger assures her, trying to stop the flow of blood from her arms and her shattered fingers. "Just, please, don't make any effort to move – keep your head up," he instructs as he searches her body for other injuries and wounds.

All Hana feels is absolute confusion. She cannot make any sense of what was happening. She doesn't comprehend who these strangers are. She cannot tell where her family is or think clearly at all.

She then remembers the explosions. Two hours had passed since the house had been bombed. All that time, they had remained buried under the rubble while rescue men struggled frantically to break through the cement walls of the house to reach them. As Hana slowly starts to grasp her reality, the pain she was in intensifies.

As she is pulled from the debris, she sees the rescue workers still scouring for survivors. She pleads tearfully, "My father, mother, and little brother are there, please find them."

Bodies are unearthed from the rubble, and Hana is faced with the task of identifying her loved ones. Just a week earlier, they had been planning her future together. Hana couldn't fathom life without her family. In the rescue, Hana's little brother's lifeless body was found. She sees her little brother's face matted with blood and dust as strangers try to clean him up. The bodies of her parents are retrieved next. Their faces no longer carry any resemblance of features.

She begs to their lifeless bodies, "Please don't leave me alone. I can't live without you!"

Hana is grappling with the haunting question of why she lived while her family perished. She lost her home and family in a single day. She wants to have died with them. Seeing the bodies pulled from the rubble, a cold realization creeps through her - they might have survived if she hadn't been bound to a wheelchair.

Part 2 (Al-Karama)

Aisha's eyes sparkle with joy as she catches sight of her mother, who stands welcomingly, inviting her into a warm embrace. She starts running toward the comforting hug she knows so well. But suddenly, the deafening roar of airplanes fills the air, making Aisha stop in her tracks. She looks up at the sky, her heart pounding with fear, a tightness gripping her chest. When she turns back to her mom, she's gone. Aisha is left with a sense of deep longing ensconced in an eerie silence. The distant hum of airplanes disrupts her dreams.

Aisha's eyes flutter open, and the room around her at Al-Karama Kids Home comes into focus. At this Gaza orphanage, she and other children sleep each night. Rows of single beds stretch out before her.

Each bed has a side table containing a colourful water bottle and a soft toy, most of which are teddy bears. She looks at the cotton doll sitting on her side table. The sight brings a faint smile to Aisha's lips.

Her gaze drifts to the long wall cupboard, stretching across the room, where the children store their belongings. It stands like a silent guardian, watching over the room and its occupants at night. In the dim light filtering through the windows, she sees the tall stack of blankets, kept in one corner. With a sigh, Aisha stretches and swings her legs over the edge of her bed. She sees Hana sleeping in a cot next to her. Her wheelchair is leaning against the wall by her bed. She feels a gaze upon her and turns to see Amal looking at her in the darkness. Amal arrived at Al-Karama a week ago. In the dim glow of the orphanage's night lights, children squirm in bed, pulling their blankets tight, hushed whispers filling the room.

Every time Aisha wakes up from her sleep, Amal talks to her. They talk about their lost homes and lost families. Amal shares her worst fears with Aisha. "Whenever I hear ambulance sirens," she says, "I can't help but cry. I heard so many of them during the war." Amal lost her whole family in an airstrike; she can't remember them anymore. The only thing she remembers is the sound of ambulance sirens.

Most kids at Al-Karama don't sleep. They're always scared. The overhead sound of airplanes sends Aisha's heart racing. The sound triggers memories of loss and fear. Every night as Aisha lies in her small bed, the soft embrace of sleep takes her to a place where her mother still exists. In her dreams, she feels the warmth of her mother's kisses and hugs. It's a fleeting moment of solace that disappears with the dawn, leaving Aisha with a sense of longing. In her darkest moments, she wishes to die so she can go to her mother. Aisha arrived at Al-Karama several years ago after her father, mother, and brother were killed in an Israeli airstrike.

At Al-Karama Children's Home in Gaza City, the bright walls of the orphanage try to conceal the scars etched by the conflict outside. The common room feels warm and cozy, with colourful rugs and cushions on the floor. Sunlight peeks through curtains decorated with artwork, lighting up shelves of books and toys. Children sit on the floor, drawing and colouring in their sketchbooks. One can hear the soft scratch of coloured pencils on paper and the occasional giggle as they work.

Ahmed sits on a cushion, legs curled under him. Ahmed's fingers clutch the crayons tightly as he draws. His brows furrow with concentration, his hand shaking slightly with each stroke. Every now and then, he lets out a frustrated sigh. Ahmed's crayon strokes tell a vivid story of war-rockets soaring into the sky, fighter jets roaring across the paper, and people breaking into pieces. Ahmed is not alone; many children at the kids' home draw war because that is what they know and remember.

Sitting in a corner is an 11-year-old boy, Bilal, staring at the floor. Two Israeli missiles hit a beach in Gaza City this summer while Bilal was playing football with his little brother and three cousins. Bilal made it through, but sadly, the other four could not. Despite five months passing by, the memory torments him still. Since the incident, Bilal has been undergoing treatment at a mental health center. Should his appointment be postponed or if there was a delay in getting his medications, he would become uncontrollable.

Abdul, the caregiver at the orphanage, known as 'Baba' by the children, steps into the room. He walks towards Bilal, placing a hand on the boy's shoulder.

He says softly, "You've got to go to the mental health centre today, son. It's important."

"I don't want to go, Baba," says Bilal, staring at the floor. Abdul leans in, concern etched on his face. "It's for your own good, Bilal. They'll help you deal with everything." Bilal's gaze remains fixed on the floor, his hands trembling. "I don't want to do anything. I just want to kill them all." Abdul's voice remains gentle. "Son, we can't talk like that. Violence won't bring them back."

Sometimes Bilal becomes extremely violent. He breaks everything and then starts banging his head against the wall. He even tried to throw himself off the roof once. "I dream about them every night. Holding them in my arms. I'll never go to the beach again; that's where they died," Bilal says, his voice rising.

Abdul speaks softly, "We can't bring them back, Bilal. But we can't let their memories hurt us forever either. Let's go get you the help you need." Bilal remains silent, his eyes filled with a mixture of pain, anger, and the burden of a childhood lost to war.

In the rear courtyard of Al-Noor General Hospital, the scene this morning appears rather uncommon.

Dozens of children sit in rows, each with bowls filled with a variety of colourful paints and a blank white sheet in front of them. They are drawing their thoughts and dreams on paper. Youth activists have organized an art activity for the numerous children displaced by the war.

The hospital courtyard, usually sombre, is now alive with vibrant colours. Amidst a sea of makeshift tents, the children gather together, playfully jostling and sharing their artwork with one another. Laughter fills the air, briefly lifting the solemn mood in the hospital. Several of the tents are full of dead bodies recovered from war-torn regions. Oblivious to this, the children celebrate a day of joy and colour, a day to dream. It is a brief respite from the death and destruction around them.

Many children are painting flags, while others are drawing their homes. Seven-year-old Suha draws her house, not knowing if it is still standing or if it has been destroyed. Some children draw themselves playing in a park, a reminder of their former lives. Nafeeza draws her kitchen toys which she misses so much. Bilal's face lights up as he looks at his drawing, a soft curve forming at the corners of his lips. It shows him and his little brother, Zakaria, playing happily on the beach. His fingers trace the outlines of the figures he has drawn. It's a comforting moment, a break from the pain, and he feels at peace.

Close by, six-year-old Aya stands with her eyes closed, her hands folded near her chest, a grin spreading across her face as a youth volunteer gently applies red paint to her cheeks. Aya giggles as the soft bristles of the paintbrush send a tingling sensation across her face. Other youth volunteers too sprinkle a bit of magic by painting designs on the eager faces of several children—from whimsical creatures to celestial wonders like sparkling stars, the sun, and the moon. The volunteers know this will not solve their trauma, but it's a momentary distraction to uplift their moods. The painted faces bring joy, offering an escape from the chaos and brutality of the war into another world.

The war in Gaza created more than 1,500 new orphans, in addition to tens of thousands already living in Gaza, according to The UN Children's Fund UNICEF has stated hundreds of thousands of these children remain in desperate need of psychological help to overcome the long-term mental health damage the war caused.

Whispers of the Valley

"Gar firdaus, bar ruhe zamin ast, hamin asto, hamin asto, hamin ast." These timeless words of the great Indian poet Amir Khusrau capture the ethereal beauty of the Kashmir valley. For centuries, Kashmir has enchanted travellers with its breathtaking landscapes and serene charm. However, behind the serene façade of this idyllic paradise lies a world of turmoil. In recent decades, the peace and beauty of Kashmir have been marred by militant activities. The tranquillity once associated with this heavenly abode has been disrupted by conflict and unrest.

In the beautiful Kashmir Valley, surrounded by stunning Himalayan peaks, it was a calm winter morning in the village of Tangdhar. Situated in the

Kupwara district, Tangdhar was a border village near the Line of Control.

Five-year-old Nazia and her family, who lived there, awoke that morning to the cold air seeping into their home. Outside, a blanket of frost covered the fields where her father, Noor, laboured tirelessly each day to provide for his family. Nazia's mother, Hina, lit a kangri, a traditional earthen pot filled with warm embers, to stave off the morning chill. A kettle of kehwa, fragrant spiced tea, simmered on the hearth, filling the air with its invigorating aroma. Little Nazia, wrapped in her colourful phiran (traditional Kashmiri dress), played around in their cozy home. When breakfast was ready, they sat together at the low wooden table and enjoyed a simple yet hearty meal of warm flatbreads with saffron-infused honey and butter. Nazia's laughter filled their home, as pure as the fresh snow outside.

The peace in their home was abruptly disrupted by resounding knocks on the door. Their house was about 20 kilometres from the ceasefire line between the Indian and the Pakistani forces. Dense forests nearby were known for hiding fighters from Lashkar-e-Taiba. These militants often demanded food and lodging from nearby villages.

Noor's expression darkened. He spoke in a hushed tone to Hina, "Mujhe lag raha hai yeh militants hain. Humko chup karke rehna chahiye." (I think they are militants. We should stay quiet.) When no one opened the door, three militants scaled the walls and entered the compound. The armed men towered over them, demanding food and shelter for the night. Nazia hid behind her mother, who stood shivering in fear. As one of them cast a dirty glance at young Nazia, Noor, in a protective instinct, charged at him and landed a blow across his jaw. In swift retaliation, the other two militants advanced, assaulting Noor with the butts of their rifles.

Nazia's eyes widened in terror as she watched the menacing militants viciously strike her father and mother with brutal rifle butts. Loud, harsh thuds filled the room as her parents declined the intruders' request for shelter. Shivering with fear, Nazia retreated quietly and slowly, her small frame trembling with every step. Her heart racing, she walked through the dimly lit house until she reached their storage room.

The room, illuminated only by faint light seeping through the cracks, had sacks of grains and a small bed with a massive trunk underneath. It had been her favourite hiding spot during countless playful escapes from her mother's occasional scoldings. She slipped under the bed and tucked herself behind the trunk, her body still trembling with fear. Holding her breath, she squeezed her eyes shut, trying to block out the terrifying reality. The coarse wood of the bed frame pressed against her back, and the cold floor chilled her through her clothes.

As she huddled there, she could hear sounds of the militants scouring the house. Every footstep, every scrape of furniture being moved, sent a jolt of terror through her. Nazia's breath came in shallow, panicked gasps. Her heart pounded so loudly she was sure it would give her away.

Eventually, the militants, unable to locate her, left the house, leaving behind an eerie silence. Nazia could not move, her body stiff and numb. For what felt like an eternity, she stayed hidden behind the trunk, her muscles cramped and aching. Slowly, she gathered the courage to move. Her heart racing, she slid out of her hiding place. She inched her way towards the main entrance of the house, her legs weak and unsteady.

The room where they had shared breakfast just moments before was now in disarray. The breakfast table, where her mother had set their morning meal, lay overturned. Plates lay scattered, broken into pieces. The food they had enjoyed was now a mess on the ground. In the midst of this disordered scene, Nazia's eyes met the sight of her parents lying on the floor, their bodies covered in blood.

Nazia rushed towards her mother and clung to her, expecting the warmth of her mother's embrace to envelop her, as it always had. She lay down beside her, waiting for her to stir, unable to grasp the cruel tragedy that had befallen her. But her mother, forever still, would never hug her again. Her tiny hand reached out for her father's, seeking the reassurance of his firm grip—a bond they shared during village strolls and walks to her school. However, that day, his hand remained still. She could not comprehend that her father would never walk with her again.

Part 2

A group of girls wearing head scarves wait in line for their breakfast at an orphanage located on the outskirts of Srinagar, the capital of India-administered Kashmir. Every meal consists of traditional Kashmiri food. While the morning one comprises salted tea (noon chai) with traditional bread, lunch and dinner are rice with vegetables or meat curry.

Four-year-old Faiqa can't contain her growing impatience as she waits in line. Her tummy rumbles with hunger, and she doesn't resist the urge to peek ahead, hoping for a glimpse of the serving counter.

"Don't worry, little one, it's almost our turn," says Nazia, an older girl standing behind her. Since Faiqa's arrival at the orphanage a month ago, Nazia has been looking after her as if she were her own younger sister. In Faiqa, Nazia sees a poignant reminder of her own past, the way she was when she first arrived at the orphanage a decade ago.

After the tragic incident on that fateful day, Nazia's uncle, who resided in a neighbouring village, brought her here. When Nazia first arrived, she was assigned to a roomy dormitory with eleven other girls, and 'ammi' took care of her and loved her.

Kausar Bano, a young matron at the orphanage, was fondly addressed as 'ammi' by the children. Since the institution's inception, she had dedicated her life to caring for children who had lost their families. Girls who arrived in the orphanage were organized in groups of twelve. Each group had its own 'ammi' or motherly figure, who not only looked after them, bathed and fed them, but also told them bedtime stories.

Ten years ago, when Nazia first arrived at the orphanage, Kausar Bano would often find her weeping in bed during the quiet nights. The remedy for such profound grief lay in the tender love of a mother, a love that "ammi" showered upon them. The haunting memory of her lifeless parents, surrounded by a pool of blood, left Nazia speechless for weeks. However, with the affectionate care of 'ammi' and the companionship of fellow orphans, she gradually found her voice again.

Yet, even today, Nazia's smile fades at the mention of her family.

Many of the one hundred girls in the orphanage have seen the horrifying atrocities committed by militants against their families, including rape, stabbings, gunshots, and death. Every now and then, the matrons come across a child who cries throughout the night.

Afreen is one such child. The matrons weep when they see her grieve. Witnessing her mother's rape and her father's murder, six-year-old Afreen had been through unimaginable trauma. She turned into a rock and remained motionless and speechless for weeks.

The orphanage is home to girls of all ages, with the youngest being Faiqa. Every child who arrives with a broken heart heals over time. The healing is slow and painful but inevitable. The discipline and routine at the orphanage shape their lives. They attend a school attached to the orphanage, where education helps piece together their shattered lives. Their teachers often observe, "The children are sharp, and with some guidance, they can do very well. They are like ordinary children, just a little sombre."

In the quiet of dawn, as the sun's first light brushes the sky, revealing the nearby Himalayan ranges, Nazia and her friends wake up and quickly climb out of the bunk beds. Laughter and quiet conversations fill the dormitory as they get ready for the day ahead. The older girls help the little ones with their morning routine. Nazia smiles warmly at Faiqa, who is struggling with her socks, her brows furrowed in concentration. "There you go, Faiqa," Nazia says patiently. "You've almost got it. Just a little more..."

When her little foot slips into the sock at last, Faiqa's face lights up with a beaming grin, and she claps her hands in pure delight. "I did it, Keeki! (elder sister in Kashmiri) Look!" Nazia laughs as she celebrates Faiqa's small victory. With everyone dressed and ready, they make their way to the school, just in time for the morning assembly held on an open ground. The children stand in perfect rows, the order and discipline instilled by their education seamlessly integrated into their daily lives.

Once classes begin, the day passes by like a breeze for Nazia. Her favourite subjects are History and Social Science. In the brief 45-minute lunch break, the library is her go-to place where she reads profusely about current affairs and the world at large. It was among the pages of numerous Social Science books here that she nurtured her dream: to qualify for the prestigious Indian Civil Services and become a government officer.

Education at the orphanage extends beyond academics and includes essential life skills such as cooking, cleaning, and household management. Guided by counselors, the girls are encouraged to take up sports and painting to help them cope with their violent pasts. This place has beautifully chiseled their lives.

As dusk settles over the hills, following a comforting tea and snacks, the girls gather in the study room. Before joining them, Nazia steps onto the long verandah that stretches before the study room, gazing at the sun as it dips below the horizon. The sunset never fails to stir memories of a time she once knew, her family. In her mind, the warmth of her mother's embrace and the strolls with her father in the forest near their house, still lingers, a faint but precious part of her.

Soft, little arms envelop her from behind, and Nazia turns around. With a gentle smile, Nazia scoops Faiqa into her arms, and together they look at the orange-tinged sky. "See, Faiqa," she whispers, "the sun is setting now, but tomorrow holds a brand new day, filled with fresh hopes."

In that moment, Nazia nurtures a secret vow in her heart, a promise to change the world. She yearns for a world where 'little Nazias', 'little Faiqas', 'little Afreens', and countless other girls like them would experience the warmth of a loving family. Faiqa squeezes Nazia in a tight embrace, and in that bond, the promise of a better future blossoms.

> *There are about 1 million orphans in Kashmir, with many living in orphanages. These children often face psychological problems due to the conflict in the region, and their adjustment to conventional society can be challenging after leaving the institutions. – UNICEF*

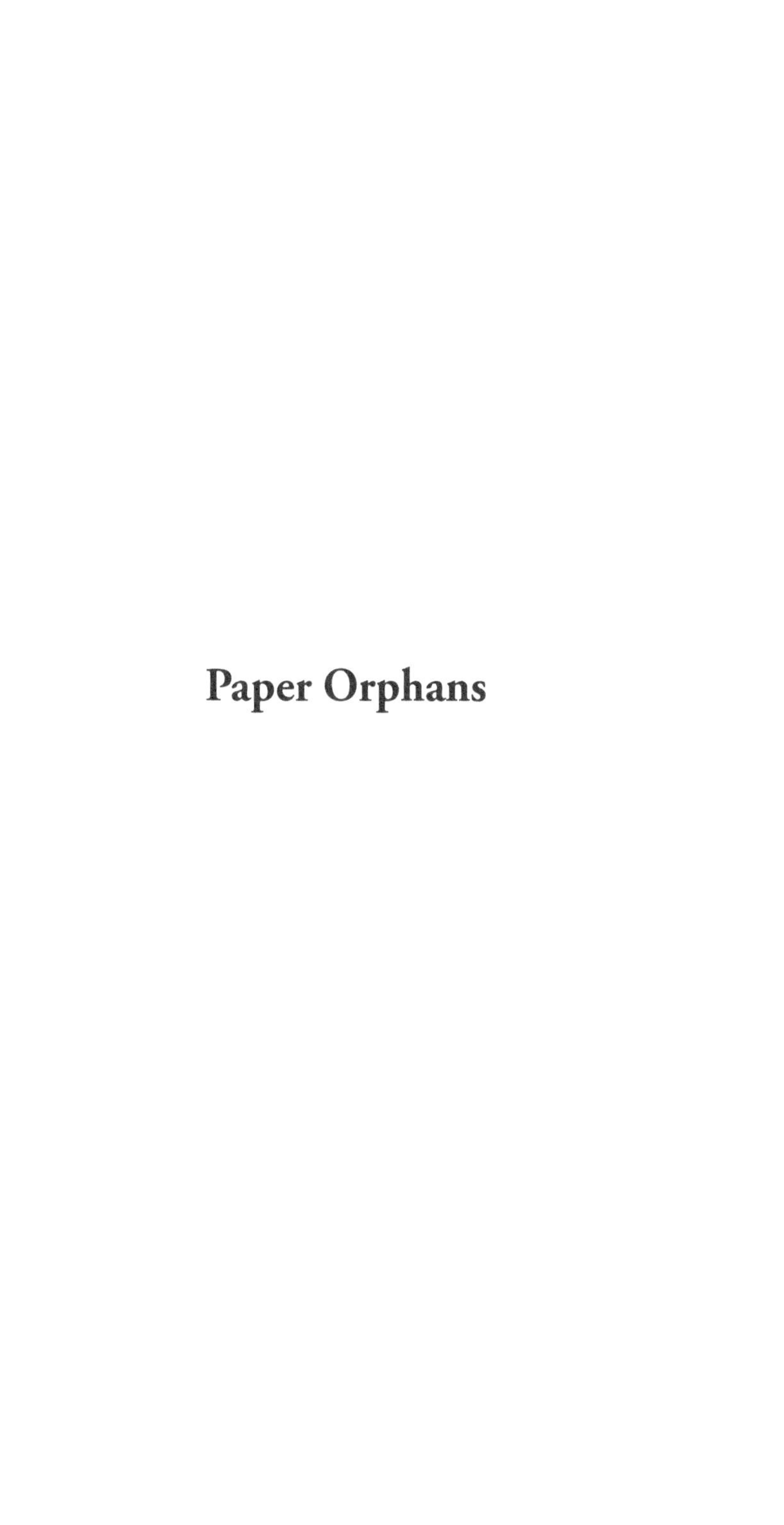

Paper Orphans

The aircraft cut through the crisp Himalayan air, its wings slicing through clouds that hung like cotton candy over the towering peaks below. Inside, Bhawana sat by a window, her eyes wide with excitement and apprehension. This was her first time flying, and the anticipation of seeing her village from the air was palpable. Beside her, Biraj and Nabin, two younger boys, pressed their faces against the same window, their breath fogging the glass. Bhawana smiled at their enthusiasm, even as her stomach churned.

As the aircraft bumped along its turbulent path, Biraj clutched his seat, his eyes wide as well with excitement and anxiety. "Wow, I can see the clouds so close!" he exclaimed.

Beside him, Nabin gripped his stomach, his face pale. "I-I don't f-feel so g-good," he murmured, his voice trembling.

Karma, their escort on the trip, moved to Nabin's side, patting his shoulder gently. "It's okay, the first time flying can be tough, especially with all these bumps," he reassured him. "I felt the same way on my very first flight."

Nabin, with a queasy expression, whispered to Bhawana, "Do you think we'll make it without getting sick?"

Bhawana managed a shaky smile. "Of course, Nabin. We're almost there. Just think about seeing our families again."

The plane continued its turbulent ride through the sky, and despite the discomfort, the children couldn't help but steal glances out the window, hoping for a glimpse of their villages below. The scene outside was breathtaking. Vast expanses of forests carpeted the land, with pristine Himalayan rivers winding through the valleys. Bhawana's heart raced as she took in the incredible sight of the mountains glowing in the morning light. For a moment, her anxiety faded into the background, replaced by a sense of wonder.

Her thoughts were interrupted as the pilot's voice crackled over the intercom, announcing their descent. As the aircraft prepared for landing over the notorious terrain of the great Himalayas, Karma grew tense. The airport was at almost 3,000 meters above sea level. The pilot barely needed to make a descent as such. Everyone except the children knew that the runway was so notoriously dangerous it had its own collection of YouTube videos of crashes, near-misses, and heart-stopping landings. The children continued to search for a hint of their villages, as the aircraft got closer to the capital of Humla, Simikot. Karma closed his eyes for a few seconds.

10 Days Ago

The telephone rang in the small post office of Samagaun, a remote village in the northern part of Nepal, its bell disturbing the silence. The postmaster, accustomed to the occasional messages that came through from the outside world, picked up the receiver. On the other end was a voice delivering important news from Kathmandu.

"Hello, this is a message for Pabitra," the voice said. "Her daughter, Bhawana along with two other children, Biraj and Nabin will be returning home from Kathmandu next week. They are to be picked up at Simikot."

The postmaster's eyes widened in surprise. He quickly made a mental note to inform Pabitra as soon as possible.

Samagaun was a village in the northern part of Nepal in the Manaslu region. The village was surrounded by mountains, including Mount Manaslu, which was the eighth-highest peak in the world. Here, journeys were measured in day's walks rather than kilometers, so rugged was the terrain. Most people in Samagaun had never lived anywhere else; their lives were framed by the peaks and valleys.

Bhawana's mother was one of them. She was small, sure-footed, and strong but tired after years of working as a porter. She earned money from farming and carrying heavy loads on her back along the precarious tracks between remote Himalayan villages. Her husband was a frail man who, due to a sickness in childhood, was unable to do heavy work. There was little medical care in these deep folds of the Himalayas — three of her six children had died of illness in infancy. She too had a list of aches and pains from years of working and walking these mountains.

On a usual day in the village a few years ago Pabitra had returned from her work to find her sister-in-law Maya visiting. Bhawana, Pabitra's eldest daughter, busied herself with making tea as Maya shared news of an agency in Kathmandu that offered education and a chance at a better life for children from remote and impoverished villages like theirs.

"I'm thinking of sending my son Vishnu," Maya had announced, "and I remember you mentioning your wish for Bhawana's education."

Pabitra's eyes shone as she listened. Education was something she had always longed for, for her children but couldn't provide in the isolated confines of Samagaun. With Maya's encouragement and the promise of opportunity in Kathmandu, Pabitra made a life-changing decision.

Despite the hardships and uncertainties, Pabitra resolved to send Bhawana to Kathmandu. It meant saving every penny while sacrificing comforts. Yet, for the chance at a better life and education, Pabitra was willing to make any sacrifice.

It had been a chilly afternoon when Bhawana arrived in Kathmandu along with two other girls. On the way to the city, Bhawana had dreamt of becoming a teacher after completing her education. She wanted to go back to her village and educate children like her. Then her mother wouldn't have to work anymore, and she would be taking care of her family.

However, her hopes started to fade the moment she set eyes on what was supposed to be their refuge for the coming years. Instead of a proper building, she was greeted by a structure that was half house and half cattle shed. Inside, there were no rooms—just clothes scattered everywhere and a makeshift kitchen in one corner. She met some kids her age and two little boys who were crying. Later, she found out they were hungry and hadn't eaten for hours. The first night, they slept on foam spread on the ground with the smell of animal dung all around. What they had hoped would be a better life turned into a nightmare. For the next six months, the children were neglected, abused, and exploited to elicit donations from tourists.

When the COVID-19 emergency began, the owners of the orphanage shut up shop. The children whose families lived nearby were sent straight home, with no planning or preparation. But Bhawana and two other little boys, whose families lived hundreds of miles away over the mountains, were virtually abandoned and left to fend for themselves for weeks. They had to prepare their own food and walk alone to seek medical help at a local hospital when needed. They would lie awake at night, listening to the distant sounds of animals, unsure of how far away they were. The two young boys, Biraj and Nabin, would cry the whole day. Bhawana looked after them like an elder sister. They were always hungry or sick.

When the Nepali child protection authorities discovered what had happened, they asked The Himalayan Innovative Society (THIS) to look into the matter. The three children were orphans who had living parents. They were "paper orphans", made so only by their fraudulent documentation.

One day Bhawana and the two boys, both from Samagaun, were rescued and taken to a transit home in Kathmandu, operated by THIS. The children were asked questions about their families and villages so the reintegration officers could trace their past. It was a long and complicated process. Biraj and Nabin were so traumatized by their time in the illegal orphanage that they refused to speak. They could hardly remember their home and their parents. THIS finally managed to track down and contact the respective parents, and prepared everyone to be reunited.

Finally, the day came when Bhawana, Biraj and Nabin could begin their journey home. Bags were packed and beds were stripped. The children wore warm scarves and hats to protect against the cold, and each carried a small bundle of food for the long journey back to Samagaun. It would take two flights and at least a day's walk before they reached their villages.

The children were introduced to a dedicated social worker called Karma. With long experience of reuniting children from orphanages with their families, he had come to accompany them to the airport and then to their villages. They were all smiling with nervousness and excitement. On the way, Karma answered their questions and talked to them about what to expect when they arrived, how living in a family was different from living in an orphanage.

Present Day

Karma opened his eyes as, with a gentle thud, the plane touched down on the runway. The flight had landed safely. The children waited patiently for their parents to arrive, from morning till evening.

When at last Bhawana saw her mother walking up the passageway. she rushed forward, bowing at her mother's feet. Pabitra embraced her daughter, tears rolling down her cheeks.

The reunion was bittersweet. The children had returned to a life their parents didn't want for them. Pabitra had paid several months' earnings to send her daughter to the capital city, and trusted she'd be looked after and given an education. Now she wondered if it had been worth it. When Bhawana told her of the awful conditions at the illegal orphanage, Pabitra's heart dropped. Her plans for her daughter had unravelled, she realized in a mixture of sadness, regret and frustration.

"I thought you were studying, so I didn't cry," Pabitra said, holding her daughter's hands. "I used to miss you a lot, but I wanted you to get an education."

Bhawana was worldlier after her time in the city. When she and her mum went to sign the documents confirming her return, Bhawana signed her name, but Pabitra could only leave a thumbprint.

Together, mother and daughter began the walk from Simikot back to their village of Samagaun. Two local women joined the hike with Bhawana leading the way. Her face was peaceful as she walked the tracks of the valley with her mother.

Below, the river thundered, while the steep hillsides soared above. It was achingly beautiful. As they walked, women on the flat rooftops of their huts, busy drying produce, greeted them warmly. Houses built from mud bricks and timber planks seemed to cling to the mountainside, surrounded by cascading green terraces. Life here was fragile and precarious. Farmers were stocking up supplies for the harsh winter months when snow would isolate the region. Livestock grazed peacefully on the slopes, with rugged peaks, veiled in mist, towering in the background.

Pabitra and Bhawana walked hand in hand much of the way, their closeness returning with every step down the familiar path home. Bhawana told her younger sisters about her experiences in the city. They failed to understand her; they were simply happy that their sister was home again.

The reintegration officers would monitor Bhawana for the next three to five years. Funding would be provided for her to attend the local school so she could receive an education while being safe with her family.

For now, it's just the simple pleasures. Bhawana stands in front of the house, basking in the golden light as the sun rises above the hills. She and her sisters play a traditional game, their laughter and chatter filling the air. This is home at last.

Every year hundreds of Nepali children are turned into "paper orphans" just because their parents cannot care for them and work at the same time. Perhaps as many as 60% of Nepal's "orphans" are economic orphans and should not be in institutions, but in day care. – UNICEF

Wounded Birds

Part 1

It is a hot and sultry morning in the village of Kibera, Africa. The scorching sun beats down on the earth, and the occasional gust of wind stirs the loose soil, carrying it in swirling patterns. Surrounded by arid land, the village does not have much vegetation to boast of. Small huts, constructed from dried grass, mud and clay, stand randomly scattered. Some roofs, partially repaired, have gaps that allow the sun to creep through.

One particular hut has a door painted in a fading shade of blue. The final coating has never been applied; the painter, the man of the house, succumbed to the AIDS virus two months ago. He now lies buried a few yards from his home.

Inside the hut, his wife lies on a mat. Nia stares blankly at the ceiling. The hut feels emptier without her husband, filled with a silence that has become a part of their lives.

Two years ago, her world had crumbled when he, the father of her two children, fell ill. Each day, Nia watched as his strength faded, his laughter quietened by pain. After a few agonizing months, he was no more. Nia, a devout believer, had clung to her faith, believing that God would protect them. But faith alone couldn't shield their family from the devastating impact of AIDS. A few months later, she tested positive as well. Now, her body is too weak even for the daily chores of her home.

The children's laughter outside contrasts sharply with the sober mood inside the hut. Nia listens, a smile tugging at her lips, remembering better days. She recalls the strong man her husband once was, the pillar of their family, now reduced to a memory and a grave just a stone's throw away.

Amina, the elder of her two children, pours water from a big container into a pan. Her young hands shake from the weight of the water. The water will soon be set to boil, a vital task in this household. Her mother will need it after some time. Their village, Kibera, is only a few miles from the main town, but even basic utilities like running water and electricity have yet to reach them.

In another corner of the hut, Amina's younger brother, Kwane, sits on the hard-packed earth which was their floor. He is busy scribbling lines on a tattered notebook, a precious possession, the only one he has. Kwane looks up with pale eyes and asks, "Aren't we going to school today?"

Amina doesn't utter a word but swiftly gets to her feet. From a corner of their hut, she picks up two empty buckets, one in each hand, and turns to Kwane. "Now hurry, or we'll be late for school." The worry never leaves her eyes as she casts a lingering glance at their mother, who lies still on the thin mat.

As they step outside, the prickly heat from the sun hits them immediately. The path before them is dusty and the air simmers with heat. They walk past other villagers engaged in their own morning routines. Children run barefoot, and women carry baskets on their heads.

The nearest stream is located approximately half a kilometer from their home. They follow the well-worn path, their bare feet brushing against the dry and dusty ground, leaving faint imprints behind. The sun beats down relentlessly, making the journey feel longer than it is. Finally, they reach a narrow ribbon of clear water glistening under the sun.

Amina dips the small buckets one by one, filling them to the brim. The cool water provides a momentary relief from the heat. Once both the buckets are filled, she places one on Kwane's head and lifts the other to her own. As they begin their journey back home, Kwane stumbles slightly before adjusting to the added weight. Sweat trickles down his forehead, but he presses on, determined not to spill a drop. Upon reaching their dwelling, Kwane gently lowers his bucket to the ground and, with all the strength he can muster, helps his sister put down hers.

Amina carefully pours the water into a small tub. Kwane climbs in, and as the cool water splashes against his skin, his eyes sparkle with excitement. Amina hands him a small, white bar of soap, and he cannot hide his surprise.

"Look, we have soap!" she says quietly.

"We really have soap?" he asks, grinning. Such moments of simple joy are scarce in their lives and the children rarely get to smile nowadays.

"Can you make some tea and give me my medicine?" Their mother's frail voice trembled from the other room.

Amina got up and gently assured her mother, "Don't worry, Mama, I'll make the tea and bring your medicine right away." In a deeply patriarchal society, the burden of managing household chores and caring for the children falls heavily upon Amina, the eldest daughter. She bears the weight of responsibility on her young shoulders, her childhood slipping away like grains of sand. Everyday she washes the dishes, prepares the fire, and cooks for the family. Her mother doesn't even want her to play with her friends.

After washing and cleaning himself, Kwane holds up a shirt in his hands. "No, not that one," says Amina, shaking her head. They are preparing for another day at school. Amina gets dressed and helps her brother comb his hair, her movements brisk but tender. Taking over the responsibilities of their mother is tough for her, a constant reminder of their altered lives. They silently eat a hasty meal of thick cornmeal porridge, commonly known as pap.

They head off to school after finishing their breakfast. The school building stands on open ground, its walls made of bricks and clay plastered with cement. The roofing consists of corrugated metal sheets, with several rectangular classrooms featuring open-air verandas and windows without glass, allowing natural light and air to circulate freely.

By the time they reach the school grounds, other students have already gathered for the morning assembly. Kwane and Amina enjoy singing the morning prayer with everyone; it gives them a sense of belonging. In class, Amina is a bright student, but she has kept a secret from their teachers. She hasn't mentioned that their father has passed away, and their mother is unwell. Amina is afraid that if her school finds out, they might say unkind things due to the stigma surrounding AIDS. Kids might tease them, saying, "Your father died of AIDS, so you might too." and that thought terrifies Amina. She doesn't want her friends to avoid them because of these misconceptions.

After school, Kwane hurries to the back of the schoolyard, where the pit latrine stands against a backdrop of overgrown bushes. As Kwane approaches, the pungent odor of human waste mingles with the earthy scent of decay, filling the air. The pit itself, a dark abyss at the center of the latrine, emits a foul odor that makes Kwane's stomach churn. Despite the discomfort and the unhygienic conditions, Kwane knows this is the only option for answering nature's call during school hours. His heart pounds with fear every time he enters the latrine, his mind haunted by the possibility of slipping and falling into the grim pit below. This is a challenge faced by many schools in Africa, where access to clean water and proper sanitation facilities remains a distant dream for countless students.

As Amina and Kwane return from school, their weary faces light up with surprise when they hear a familiar voice inside their small hut. They hurriedly step inside, their school bags slung over their shoulders. There, sitting on a makeshift stool near their mother's bed, is Sister Kemi. A compassionate woman, she is a nun at the local convent and a social worker at the nearby hospital. She has made it her life's mission to help families devastated by the AIDS virus. Her warm, caring eyes sparkle behind her large round spectacles as she glances up at the children.

"Hello, Amina and Kwane," Sister Kemi greets them with a gentle smile. "I hope you had a good day at school."

Amina nods, "Yes, Sister Kemi. It was a good day. How is Mama doing?"

Their mother, lying on a thin mattress, manages a weak smile and beckons them closer. "I'm feeling a little better today, my darlings," she whispers.

Kwane, with his eyes wide, asks Sister Kemi, "Sister, what were you talking to Mama about?"

Sister Kemi's expression grows solemn as she replies, "We were discussing some important things, my dear. Your mother and I were talking about the grant money and how it will help your family. We're working together to ensure you have everything you need."

Sister Kemi has been helping them for many months since their mother was first diagnosed, partly by registering them for grants. But to collect the grant money, Amina's mother has to leave home at 4 am in the morning and walk three miles into town despite her weakened body. Their family relies solely on this money to survive.

Amina's brows furrow with worry as she glances at her mother's pale face. "Will Mama be okay, Sister?" she asks.

Sister Kemi, with a somber expression, hands over the regular medicines. Her mother has never received the proper anti-AIDS drugs that could offer some respite. The available medicines are just cocktails of painkillers, vitamins, and antibiotics, trying to keep the worst of the symptoms at bay. As a result, for her, time is measured in months rather than years.

Tears well in Sister Kemi's eyes as she embraces Amina. Amina's mother instructs in a weak voice, "If something happens to me, promise you'll turn to Sister Kemi." After a pause, she continues, "She will take care of you, just like a mother."

The children burst into tears. The mere thought of life without their mother is unbearable. At night, Amina lies awake, her mind plagued by fears of the unknown. She shudders at the superstitions rampant in their community, aware of the dangerous belief that having sex with a virgin could cure AIDS. This belief has exacerbated the AIDS epidemic in Africa, leading to a devastating increase in the transmission of the disease.

Sister Kemi smiles warmly at the children. "I'll continue to do everything I can to support you and your family. You're not alone in this, and we'll face these challenges together as a community."

Several million children have already been orphaned by South Africa's AIDS epidemic. In most cases, extended families intervene and take responsibility for raising the orphans. But in small towns like Kibera, there aren't enough living adult relatives left to cope. Many of Amina's relatives have already died of AIDS. The only consistent adult presence in their lives is Sister Kemi.

The week following Sister Kemi's visit, Amina's mother falls very ill and has to be taken to the hospital. The children visit their mom, but she cannot speak. Alone and vulnerable, the two of them begin to cry. When their mother is in the hospital, they are completely on their own. People in the village know that their father is dead and their mother is sick, but they don't care. No one bothers to visit them or console them. The missionaries have taken in some orphans recently, but as long as their mother is alive, Amina and Kwane remain alone.

One week after their mother's admission to the hospital, Amina and Kwane find themselves orphaned by AIDS. Their mother is laid to rest next to their father a few meters from their home. Tradition demands that the children look upon their mother's face one final time before saying their farewells. Silent sobs shake their small frames as they cling to each other for comfort. The village witnesses more and more burials each month, and the number of fresh mounds of earth in the graveyard keeps growing, each new grave a stark reminder of the disease's unyielding grip.

As the sun dips below the hills, a chilling realization settles over the village. AIDS, a devastating plague, has cast a long and somber shadow over the lives of children who will carry the burden of its legacy for generations to come.

Part 2

It is late afternoon as Sister Kemi enters the missionaries' convent gate, holding Amina and Kwane's hands tightly. As they step through, the harmonious sound of hymns being sung in unison fills the air. Sister Kemi leads them to the chapel, where a congregation of nuns, much like herself, kneels on one side, and a small group of children kneels together on the other. Amina and Kwane join the children, their voices trembling as they attempt to sing the hymns. Tears well up in their eyes as they think about their mother.

That evening, Sister Kemi gently tucks Amina and Kwane into bed in one of the convent's small, simple rooms. "Rest well, children," she says, her voice tender. "Tomorrow is a new day."

The following morning, Amina and Kwane sit on the edge of their bed, clutching the soft fabric of their blankets in their hands. Sister Kemi enters the room and sets down two plates of fresh bread and two glasses of milk on the bedside table. "Time to get ready," she says gently. "We have a long journey ahead."

As they pack their few belongings into a small bag, Amina and Kwane exchange glances. They want to stay at the convent with Sister Kemi. They follow her through the quiet halls, the scent of freshly baked bread wafting from the kitchen. Sister Kemi leads them to her car, parked under the shade of a large acacia tree. She opens the rear door, and Amina and Kwane slide into the back seat, their bags resting on their laps.

They are going to Harmony House, a family-run orphanage and school that shelters around 200 children. The convent is already at full capacity and unable to accommodate more orphans, so this transition is necessary. Sister Kemi starts the car, and soon they are on a straight, dusty road, leaving the convent behind. The sensation of being in a moving vehicle for the first time fills them with excitement. Through the car window, they glimpse rows of graves stretching alongside the road. Sister Kemi appears thoughtful throughout the journey.

As they approach Harmony House, the road gives way to a vast open expanse. The orphanage stands in an open space surrounded by lush trees. The main building is a two-story house with a red roof and big windows. The front porch has a few colorful flower pots. Next to the main house is a huge shed that's been converted into living quarters for the children. The shed also houses paintings by the children. Several small gardens surround it.

When the car slows down near the entrance, they observe a group of kids engrossed in a ball game. The children stop the play to smile and wave at Amina and Kwane. Worried as they had been about the new place and leaving Sister Kemi behind, the friendly and welcoming gestures make them feel better. "You will like it here, children," says Sister Kemi as they get out of the car.

"How many children live here, Sister?" Kwane asks, looking around with surprise. "Many of them, dear," Sister Kemi replies.

A gentle voice interrupts their conversation, and they turn to see a plump, cheery-faced woman walking toward them with a big smile. She introduces herself as Maria, the lady who runs the orphanage.

"Hello, children, how are you?" Maria asks as she hugs Amina and Kwane, her eyes reflecting deep care and compassion. Amina and Kwane feel a sense of belonging for the first time in a long while. Another woman with a rotund face, who appears to be in her early 50s, follows Maria. She is Bridget, Maria's twin sister. Maria and Bridget work together along with local volunteers to run Harmony House. Amina is surprised to see the two women looking exactly alike.

The next morning, as dawn breaks and the chirping of birds fills the silence of daybreak, some children stir beneath soft quilts in a large room filled with rows of beds. Among them are Amina and Kwane, lying side by side, fast asleep. For the first time in months, Amina sleeps peacefully, free from the worries that had haunted her nights.

Bridget begins her morning rounds, gently waking the children. Maria sits up in a bed next to that of another boy. As she rises, a young woman named Nala, who helps with the children, brings her a mug of coffee. Maria places the coffee on the side table and checks the boy's forehead. "Juma seems to have a mild fever. Please bring the thermometer," she says to Nala.

In Harmony House, they live like one big family. Another boy has a cold, so Nala gives him cough syrup, singing a soothing tune. Other children join in, clapping and singing to welcome the new arrivals. Amina and Kwane, now awake, observe the scene with wide eyes. The warm smiles and gentle care around them bring a sense of comfort they hadn't felt in a long time. It's a new world for them, far from the life-threatening after effects of a terrible disease that takes away loved ones, and a place more secure than their own home.

Nearly eight o'clock in the morning, and more than 200 kids are waiting in a disorganized line for breakfast. Kwane and Anina join the children's group and experience everything with fresh eyes. Every kid holds a worn and dented metal plate. The children, some talking softly, pass the time by tracing patterns in the dirt. Some adults hastily serve the children as they wait in line. Each plate is filled with steaming corn porridge using a spoon. It's a meager meal by many standards, but in this place, it's a lifeline.

After eating breakfast, a crowd of kids surround Bridget and Maria in an open field with a couple of see-through polyethylene greenhouses nearby. The children are excited to get started on planting new seedlings. The greenhouses contain carefully cultivated dark soil to create a nurturing plant environment.

With a doll by her side, a young girl named Zahara kneels in the soft earth, her small fingers digging into the soil. Kneeling beside her is Amina. "Your doll is really nice," Amina says softly.

Zahara smiles and says in a small voice, "I like bananas and apples." Two years ago, she had been sexually assaulted by three men. When she arrived at Harmony House, her body had been covered in pus. Night after night, fear kept Zahara wide awake, dreading the return of those monsters. She spoke quietly to avoid being heard and taken away. Maria never left her side, night after night. It took her months to recover, Even now she occasionally wakes up screaming at night. Many children residing at Harmony House have been victims of rape. As Amina and Zahara dig into the soil to plant seeds, they feel a connection with the earth. The earth has a unique ability to heal their wounds and provide answers to their profound questions.

Among the children, a 12-year-old boy named Nabil is planting saplings. The young boy had recently laid his mother and the rest of his family to rest. His baby brother too was gone. His sister, a mere 6-year-old, is his only remaining connection to his past. Recently, he tested positive for AIDS.

Kwane stands by his side, observing him with keen interest. Soon, Nabil shows him how to water the newly planted saplings. Kwane smiles. He likes the feeling of cool water on his hands.

On another side of the open ground is a play area where Thandi, an imaginative 9-year-old, is engaged in a game of storytelling with Sam. Thandi has been living with HIV since birth and has faced her share of challenges. Her best friend, Sam, is an 11-year-old boy who loves Thandi and shares her exciting stories with others, often drawing more children into their imaginative world. In that instant, differences between HIV-positive children and others don't matter. It becomes a place where everyone feels accepted and understood.

However, the orphanage is running out of space, with new children arriving every day, and no one is turned away. The Harmony House kids share everything with each other. From day one, Bridget and Maria have taught them to live like one big family, where everyone helps everyone. All the children feel safe and loved living here. Maria and Bridget look after them as their own. Every child who is traumatized by the past is supported at Harmony Home. Here, they grow up together, taking care of the younger ones. The shared bond among them is the loss of their parents.

As evening falls, the sound of drums and singing wafts through the air. Two men, local musicians who often come visiting, play their songs to dance with the children. They are fond of Maria and Bridget. It is their way of contributing to their own people. A large group of children has gathered around them. Amina gets excited and starts dancing. She always gets the moves right. Kwane is shy at first but soon joins in as well. Maria and Bridget are not far behind them.

Inspired by the lively tunes, the children start moving gracefully. Some of them begin to perform their favourite dance moves. With arms extended, mimicking birds spreading their wings, they glide across the open ground. In that moment, they resemble wounded birds attempting to rise above the ground and ascend into the vast blue sky, seeking to reclaim their lives.

More than 11 million children under the age of 15 in sub-Saharan Africa have lost at least one parent to HIV/AIDS; 34 million children have been orphaned overall. Eighty percent of all the world's children orphaned by HIV/AIDS reside in sub-Saharan Africa – UNICEF

Lost Childhood

The sun sets over the arid plains of the Zhari Dasht Camp in southern Afghanistan. The air is dusty, and the earth is parched. The camp, a sprawling maze of tents and mud huts, sits amidst the dry landscape. Dust and sand swirl through the air, whipped up by the occasional gust of wind. The terrain here is flat and barren, with only a few scraggly bushes dotting the horizon, standing in stark contrast to the majestic mountains that loom in the distance.

Families displaced by the relentless fighting in southern Afghanistan now call this camp home. They have fled from their villages and towns, seeking refuge from the violence that has uprooted their lives.

Outside one of the tents, four young girls play in the dirt. They laugh and giggle as they draw circles with a stick and take turns jumping into them. The youngest, barely two years old, has no idea that soon, she will be taken away from her family to stay with strangers. Her father, Fahim, has sold her to an Afghan living abroad.

Nearby, seven-year-old Zahra, with her dark eyes and rosy cheeks, giggles with her friends. Her laughter fades as she enters her hut with dirt walls, where the harsh reality hits her: she has been sold as a child bride. Her father received 200,000 Afghanis (about $2,200) in the form of sheep, land, and cash from Omar, a 55-year-old man with white eyebrows and a thick beard.

For four years, Zahra's family has lived in this displacement camp, enduring poverty and helplessness. International aid has dried up, and the country's collapsing economy means they can't afford basic necessities like food. With no work and no money, selling his children has become Fahim's only option.

Fahim sits cross-legged on a torn mat, his face etched with worry. "Zahra, come here," he calls. Zahra approaches hesitantly.

"Do you know why I did it?" Fahim asks, his voice breaking.

Zahra shakes her head, tears welling up in her eyes.

"The man who bought you... he says he will look after you. He has a wife who will care for you like her own child," Fahim tries to assure her.

"But he is old, Baba. What if he hurts me?" Zahra's voice trembles.

"I had no choice, Zahra. We have no food, no money. If I didn't sell you, we would all starve," Fahim explains. Fahim is under no illusions about what the sale means for his daughter – or what the grim situation means for his family's future. Omar said he would use her as a worker, not a bride, but Fahim knows he has no control over what happens to her now. Omar told him, "I'm paying for the girl. It's none of your business what I'm doing with her… that's my business."

Meanwhile, outside the tent, a mother cradles her seven-month-old baby, recently sold to pay medical debts. She is nerve-racked, unable to sleep at night, haunted by the cries of her child. In another tent, Roya sold her one-month-old daughter, who was still breastfeeding, to an Afghan family, but the baby wouldn't stop crying, so they returned her. Roya did not get any money. Now, she is trying to sell her other two daughters, who are two and four years old.

As international aid dwindles and the country's economy collapses, families in rural areas of Afghanistan find themselves with nothing left to sell but their children. Most of the girls have been sold just to buy food. Some end up with families who care for them, but others, as young as ten, are sold under the guise of marriage to much older men, who can do whatever they want with them.

In one tent, a man sits with his three young daughters, all under five years old. "If I don't sell one of them, all my other children will die of hunger," he tells his friend.

A few days later, Zahra's family is preparing to say goodbye to their daughter. Zahra, dressed in a black head covering adorned with a colorful floral garland, clings to her mother, her face hidden in her mother's embrace. Her father, tears streaming down his face, tells Omar, "This is your bride. Please take care of her—you are responsible for her now. Please don't beat her."

Omar nods in agreement, then grips Zahra's arm firmly and leads her out the door. As they step outside, Zahra's parents stand by the doorway, their eyes filled with sorrow. Zahra digs her feet into the dirt, trying to resist, but Omar's grip is unyielding. She is dragged toward the waiting car, her small frame struggling against his hold.

As the car pulls away, Zahra looks back one last time at her mud hut and her family standing forlornly outside it. The distance between them grows, and the familiar sight of her home and loved ones fades into the dusty horizon.

As the effects of poverty compound in Afghanistan, nearly two-thirds of the population, including more than 15 million children, need urgent humanitarian assistance to protect themselves from hunger and disease. – UNICEF

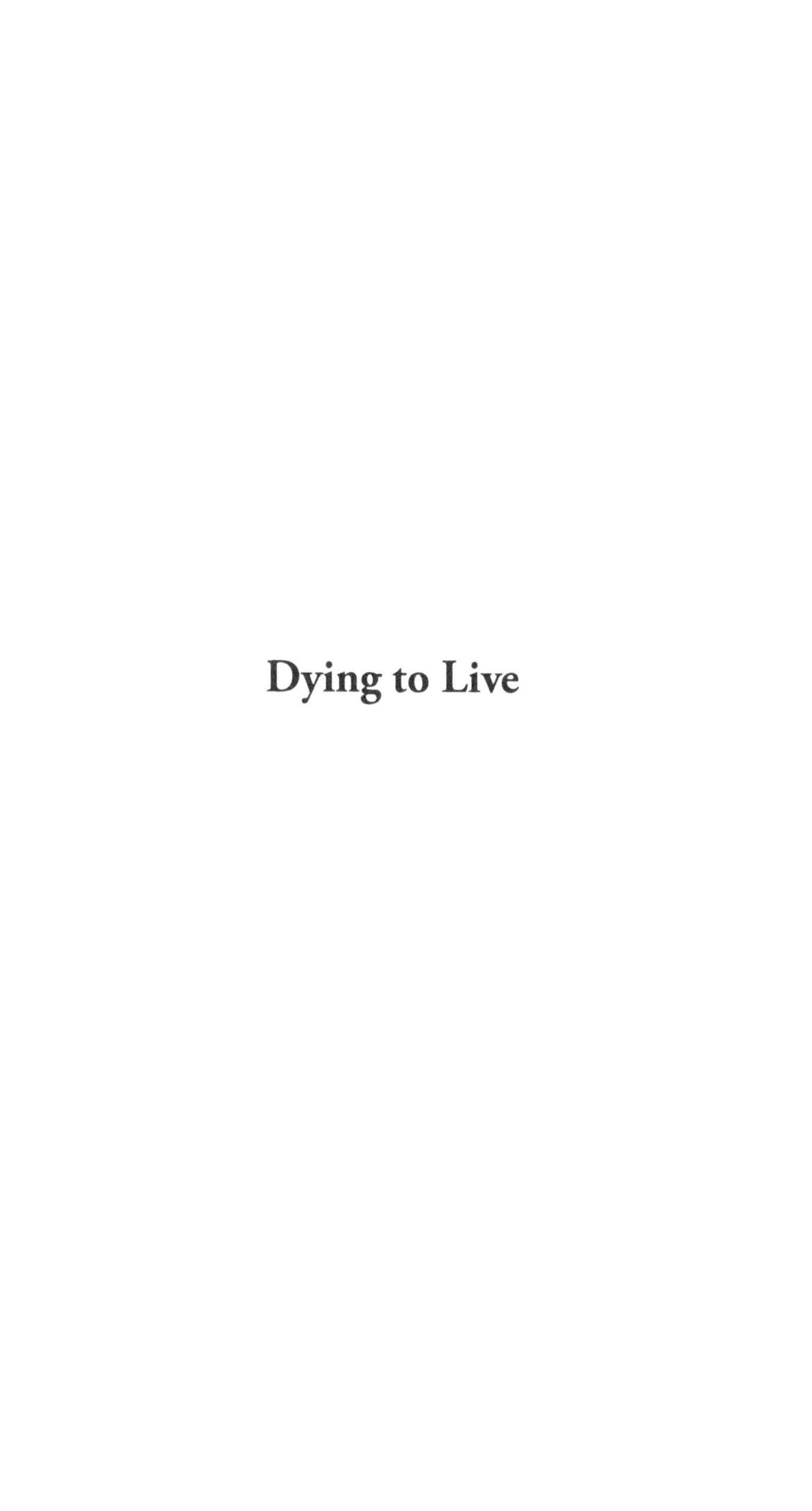

Dying to Live

Sade can never forget the night her mother died. The memory of that night haunts her day in and day out. Her mother had been ill for many months due to an infection that could not be cured. She belonged to the Hausa tribe of Nigeria, where women were known to be stronger than men. Finally, after long suffering, she succumbed to her illness. As her lifeless body lay on the floor of their small house, Sade sat on the floor, clinging to her father, a loving man who cared for his family. Sade's mother lay on a worn mat on the floor. Sade held her frail hand, her tiny fingers tracing the lines of her mother's soft skin.

Outside, the murmur of voices broke the silence. Sade could hear the shuffling of feet and the occasional cough as the village men gathered. Their hushed tones, growing louder as they discussed something. Her father stood up and went near the door, his face etched with worry and sorrow. He glanced back at Sade and her mother, took a deep breath and stepped outside.

The night air was cool, in contrast to the warmth inside the room. The men surrounded him, speaking in low, urgent tones. "We have to do something," one man said. Her father fell silent, turned back toward the house, then stepped into the room, his eyes locking onto Sade's. She saw helplessness in his gaze, something she wouldn't fully understand until years later.

He left without a word. Sade clung to her mother's body, tears streaming down her face. She cried until she couldn't cry anymore, eventually falling asleep beside the lifeless body.

Hours had passed when she woke up and saw her mother's body was gone. She soon realized that she was alone and everyone had left her. Panic surged through six-year-old Sade as she stumbled outside, calling frantically for her father. "Baba! Baba!" The village was strangely quiet. The men who had gathered were now gone. Terrified, she retreated back into the house and sat in a corner, hugging her knees, thinking about her mother and the life that had slipped away.

At dawn, as the first light of day began to stir the dusty streets into activity, Sade's father returned. However, the house felt empty without her mother. Sade ran to hug him, but he pushed her away with a rough shove. He was accompanied by two tall and stern men. His eyes, once filled with love and warmth, were now full of pain and fear. "Sade, come with us," he said. His voice was completely different from the comforting tone she used to know. "Baba, where are we going?" Sade asked, her small hand reaching for his. But he pulled away, avoiding her touch.

The men led her to a nearby church, a simple structure with peeling white paint and a small cross atop the roof. The air smelled of incense and damp wood. Inside, the church was dimly lit, with wooden benches arranged in neat rows. A faint light filtered through stained-glass windows.

"Wait here," one of the men said gruffly, pointing to a bench outside the church. Sade sat down, her legs swinging nervously. She watched as her father and the men disappeared inside. When they returned after a while, their faces were grim, and they were angrily muttering, "Ba mu da kudi da yawa" ("We do not have so much money"). Her father's shoulders slumped, and his eyes avoided hers. He turned and began to walk away.

"Baba!" Sade cried, running after him, desperation in her voice. "Don't leave me!"

He paused, his back still turned to her. "Sade, stay away from me.," he said, his voice breaking.

"Why, Baba? Why can't I come home?" she pleaded, tears streaming down her face.

Before he could answer, the two men grabbed her. "Ita mayya ce" ("She is a witch"), they spat, their voices filled with venom. To Sade, those words were meaningless yet terrifying. She was brutally attacked, enduring a relentless assault of punches and kicks. "Baba, help me!" she screamed, but her father remained still. The men finally stopped, leaving her on the dusty road, bleeding and bruised. Her father's figure faded into the distance. By then, a small crowd had formed, yet no one stepped forward to help her.

The events after that day are a blur to Sade, but she remembers sleeping on the street and begging for help. The streets of Bauchi were uneven and dusty lined with smalls and stalls with smell of refuse filling the air. Sade roamed aimlessly, relying on leftovers from strangers. No one bothered to help her. The townspeople would avoid any child accused of witchcraft.

One evening, a car pulled up to the side of the road where Sade lay, too weak to move. A Swedish aid worker named Erik, working with Safe Child Africa, was passing by. Erik saw what he thought was a dead body lying in the dirt, and he pulled over immediately. He checked to see if she was alive. By that time, a group of locals gathered nearby. One of the men said. "She's alive, but barely. She's been roaming the streets for months."

"Why hasn't anyone helped her?" Erik asked, his voice tinged with disbelief.

"She's a witch," the man replied, his tone matter-of-fact. "No one will help her."

Erik quickly lifted Sade into his arms and carried her to his car. He could feel her bones through her thin skin, and her breath was shallow. He drove quickly to the nearest hospital, praying she would survive. Sade was severely malnourished, riddled with worms, and needed daily blood transfusions. The doctors did their best to revive her. It took months of medical attention, love, and care to bring her back to health.

Sade started living with 35 other children in an orphanage run by Safe Child Africa, which works to support and protect children accused of witchcraft. The other children in the orphanage had similar experiences to Sade's. Sade got healthier by the day and even started going to school.

One day, she confided in Kamaria, a girl with whom she had formed a strong bond, saying, "I don't understand why they accused me of being a witch. I haven't done anything wrong."

"I know how you feel," Kamaria replied, tears in her eyes. "My family abandoned me, too. They said I was cursed because our crops failed. They left me in the forest. I was so scared." Sade reached out and hugged Kamaria. Finally, she found the answer to the question that had been torturing her.

In their society, all problems in life are believed to have a spiritual origin; these are generally seen as the fault of child 'witches'. This belief made her father think that Sade had been put under a spell and given the power to wreak havoc—specifically, her mother's death. That fateful day, her father had taken her to the local pastor in the church to remove the evil spirits by exorcism, but he did not have the money to pay for it. She sometimes wondered what her life would have been like if he had. But it didn't matter anymore. Even though she lost her home, she was now a happy child.

> *Safe Child Africa work with communities in Nigeria as well as international agencies to prevent the abuse of so called child 'witches.'*

Miracles

Hafsa

At the Umeed Center in Karachi, Pakistan, the phone rings on a freezing December morning. They are notified by an unknown caller about a dead body that has been abandoned near the center. The voice on the other end is hushed, almost trembling, as it speaks of a horrific discovery. Within minutes, the staffers are en route to the familiar location.

With the sun not yet up, they rely on their flashlights as they get closer to the garbage dump. At first, all they see are piles of trash, but to their shock, they discover the lifeless body of a newborn girl with her throat brutally cut by a knife. This is not the first instance of discovering deceased infant girls in that dump. There have been countless cases of unwanted babies, predominantly girls, being killed and abandoned. However, today is unlike any other morning. What they saw today is a stark reminder of the brutal realities lurking in the shadows of our society, leaving them shaken to their core.

Then, something catches their eye—a faint, almost imperceptible movement beneath a writhing mass. As the flashlight focuses on it, what they discover next turns their blood to ice. A glimpse of human flesh is visible beneath a pile of a million ants. Heartbeats quicken, breaths grow shallow. Their trembling hands push the insects aside, exposing a premature baby girl with her skin covered in ant bites. The realization quickly hits them: the babies are identical; they're twins.

They quickly wrap her in a soft, clean cloth and rush to the nearest hospital in their vehicle. In the ER, the medical staff fights to stabilize the baby. She has been stabilized after undergoing hours of surgery. According to the doctor, "It's truly miraculous that she survived." Two months later, the baby is sent to the Umeed Children's Center. The baby is named Hafsa.

Hafsa and the other abandoned babies are kept in a small, overcrowded room at the Umeed Center, with rows of closely arranged baby cots. There is a severe shortage of caregivers to meet the needs of these infants.

Despite the passing months, Hafsa doesn't start moving or crawling like other babies her age. After a year of being unable to move by herself, the caregivers decide to consult a doctor. Hafsa is diagnosed with cerebral palsy, a condition that permanently inhibits her ability to walk.

Sita

It was a hot afternoon in the small town of Katni, in the Jabalpur district of Madhya Pradesh, India. A small group of men and women had gathered outside the room of the local municipality hospital. Inside, the incessant cries of a woman could be heard. She had just given birth to a stillborn.

Ramesh, the father of the baby, stood outside the room, his face filled with sadness and disbelief. The baby had been a boy, a precious asset in their community, which still viewed girls as burdens. He was in deep shock and regret. One of the older men finally spoke, "It's time to perform the last rites." In their community, babies and young children were buried, despite the general practice of cremation in Hindu tradition.

An hour later, a few men, including Ramesh, went to a nearby field. It was a heart-wrenching sight: men all in white carrying a lifeless infant, walking through green paddy fields. With their shovels, they started digging into the hard soil. After they had dug about three feet below the ground, their shovel hit something hard.

"What was that?" one man muttered.

"Must be a rock," someone said, so they kept digging. Suddenly, there was a cracking sound, and immediately following it, the cry of a baby.

"Stop! Stop digging!" another man shouted, his voice trembling. They quickly removed the soil with their bare hands and found a broken earthen pot. Lifting it carefully, they found a tiny infant inside, moving and crying. It was a girl. She was completely shriveled up.

Ramesh stared, unable to comprehend what he was seeing. They had come to bury his dead son and instead found a living baby. "Who has buried a living baby like this?" said Ramesh, his voice trembling.

"We need to get her to the hospital," his friend said. Ramesh handed his son's body to his friends and took the crying infant.

At the local government hospital, the baby was admitted to the neonatal intensive care unit. Dr. Mehta, the attending pediatrician, immediately put her on oxygen and began treating her for hypothermia.

"She's tiny and very weak," Dr. Mehta said. "But she's alive, which is a miracle in itself."

Ramesh, still in shock, asked, "How could she survive buried below the soil?"

Dr. Mehta explained, "There might have been an air pocket inside the pot providing her with oxygen. Also, the loose soil and the pot not being made of dense clay could have allowed some oxygen to filter through. She might have survived for another hour or two if she hadn't been rescued."

When Ramesh asked how she survived without food below the soil, and how long the baby had been buried, Dr. Mehta said she might have been buried as long as "three to four days."

"She survived on her brown fat. Babies are born with fat on their abdomen, thighs, and cheeks, and they can survive on it in an emergency for some time. Once she exhausted that, she shriveled up - as you can see her now."

Ramesh felt a deep sense of destiny. He decided then and there to adopt the baby. "This is a sign," he said to himself. "God has sent her to us for a reason."

He rushed to the hospital to inform his wife, Deepa. Bursting through the door, he found her sitting in stunned silence.

"Deepa," he said, his voice trembling with grief and hope. "In the field, we found a baby girl buried beneath the soil. She was buried in a pot, but she survived."

Deepa, not yet out of her shock of losing her baby, stared at her husband. "You found her buried in the soil?"

Deepa's eyes widened in disbelief. "A girl? And she survived? How is that possible?"

"It's a miracle," Ramesh replied. "I believe God saved her life and sent her to us. Now it's our duty to do everything for her. She's fighting for her life, but once she recovers, we'll bring her home and raise her as our daughter."

Deepa immediately added, "We will call her Sita." Ramesh was in tears. Sita is a central character in the Hindu epic, the Ramayana. According to the popular mythological text, she was discovered by King Janak while he was plowing a field. Deepa embraced her husband. "I can't believe it," she whispered. "You always wanted a boy, but now you've agreed to adopt a girl. This is truly a miracle."

A year later…

On a side street, almost out of sight, a cradle swings gently in the breeze. It looks like it has been forgotten until you see the hand-painted sign in Urdu, "Don't kill the baby, leave the baby alive in the cradle." These are the cradles for the unwanted.

The cradle is one of many dotted around Karachi, part of the Jhoola, or cradle, project, which aims to prevent parents from killing and abandoning girls in garbage dumps. Baby girls are considered a curse and a financial burden, especially to poor, rural families who must cough up expensive dowries upon their marriages, while boys are usually counted upon to take care of their parents during their old age.

Mothers can leave their unwanted babies in the cradle, knowing they will be safely collected and taken care of. The Jhoola project was created by the head of the Umeed Foundation orphanage after the horrific incident in which Hafsa was found. Since the initiation of the project, the number of girls coming to Umeed has increased, and there have been fewer dead baby girls. But for poor families accepting a baby girl is very difficult. The caregivers at Umeed have to face some horrific incidents occasionally. Sometimes they find dead baby girls in the crib in front of the shelter. They suspect that families worry that, if they leave their daughter alive, someone will come looking for them to ask why they abandoned the child, or even ask them to take her back. Once a baby girl that had been left in the crib was found burned to death. She had her umbilical cord still attached, and her tiny body was fully blackened. There have been such few incidents over the years that have shaken everyone's souls, and the Umeed foundation has been dealing with such cases for a long time. But, even amid this despair, there is some hope. Umeed helps numerous girls each year to live a fulfilling life.

In the same year, on June 20th, celebrated as Children's Day in Pakistan, Hafsa is adopted by Nadia Ali, an advocate at the Karachi High Court. She had visited Umeed on Children's Day and fell in love with little Hafsa, who had blue eyes just like Nadia's mother. Later, Hafsa was treated by experts and operated on for increasing spinal curvature. With the loving care of Nadia and her husband, Hafsa grew up to be a bright young woman. She completed a graduate course in Disability Studies to prepare her to advocate for the rights of individuals with disabilities. The day Hafsa climbed the ramp of her college in Karachi in a wheelchair to receive her graduation certificate, her mother Nadia shed a silent tear of happiness sitting in the audience. All her life, she never believed in miracles, but that day she did.

Nearly 50% of the 625 million children in South Asia are girls, who face patriarchal values and harmful gender norms. – UNICEF

Prison Orphans

It is evening at one of the Hope Village orphanages in the Shunyi District of Beijing, China. A group of young children can be seen playing at a park located near a cluster of row houses. Two boys, Jun and Kai, are on the swings.

"My dad is in detention awaiting his sentence. What about yours?" asks Jun.

"He is dead," replies Kai.

"Why?" asks Jun.

"Because my mother killed him," says Kai with a pause.

"Why did your mother kill your father?"

"One day, he was very angry and hit my mother with a rod. He also used to hit me." There is a long pause, and then Kai gets down from the swing. "Where is your mother?" asks Kai to Jun.

"She died," Jun says quietly, with his head bent down. Oblivious to Jun, his father will be sentenced to death next month. With one parent dead and the other in prison, both the children have lost their homes forever.

The boys fall silent. They stop playing. It's dark already, and Jun and Kai start walking toward the community dining hall. On the way, they meet Chen, who is carrying a bag of medical supplies. Chen takes care of the village's daily operations. When Chen waves to the boys, the boys smile back and wave slowly.

Hope Village is a home for over 100 children of incarcerated parents, aged from 1 year to 18 years. Grandma Li, a strong woman in her sixties, is the head of the village. All the children look up to her as their grandmother. Grandma Li has dedicated her life to providing a nurturing environment for the children, ensuring that each child receives proper care, education, and emotional support. She organizes activities that help the children heal from their traumas, fosters a sense of community and belonging, and works closely with social workers and educators to meet the children's needs.

During dinner time, Jun and Kai sit at a table with other children in a large hall. Among the children are three girls, whom everyone finds interesting because they look exactly the same. They are triplets, and Grandma Li had told everyone when they arrived for the first time at the orphanage. The seven-year-old triplets, Fang, Ling, and Qing, have been without their mother for a year. Their father was unemployed and abusive; he often drank and beat his family. One day, when their mother could take it no more, she killed him. The girls, who were just five years old at the time, witnessed their mother killing their father.

When their mother went to prison, the girls stayed at their uncle's place. But after some time, their uncle's family started hating them, projecting their resentment for the parents onto the children. When they arrived at Hope Village, they would cry all day long, missing their mother. But slowly, with the help of Grandma Li and the other children, they began to adjust. Gradually, they started playing with the other children and began attending school every day. On Sundays, all the children worked at the village farm.

It is another day at the farm on a Sunday morning for the children of Hope Village. Fang, Ling, and Qing giggle and laugh as they help the older children pluck tomatoes from plants and put them in small baskets. The younger children use small baskets, and the older ones use bigger ones. Yan, an older girl, is supervising the group plucking tomatoes.

"Look at these tomatoes," says Fang, holding up a ripe one.

Ling and Qing smiled as they looked at the bright red tomatoes. "Yan, can we keep some for ourselves?" Qing asks, her eyes wide. "Of course, you can have some," Yan replies with a smile. "You all did a great job today." Once collected in baskets, they carry the baskets and load them onto a truck. Chen then drives everyone back. That evening, after dinner, Grandma Li talks to Fang, Ling, and Qing. Tomorrow is a big day for them. They will be visiting their mother at the town prison.

The next morning, the triplets are up early; they are excited to meet their mother. Yan helps the girls get dressed. An hour later, after breakfast, Grandma Li is driving with Fang, Ling, and Qing in the car. The triplets, dressed in identical frocks, sit in the back seat, each holding a basket of cherries from the farm.

They arrive at the prison, a tall building surrounded by high walls and barbed wire. The girls hold Grandma Li's hand tightly as they walk through the long corridors. The prison is stark and cold; the walls are painted a dull gray. They are led to a waiting room, where they sit anxiously with the basket of cherries on their lap. In a while, the door opens, and their mother enters. Min, a woman in her late twenties wearing a blue dress that hangs loosely on her thin frame, looks older than her age. Her eyes are dull, filled with a deep sadness.

The children suddenly become very quiet. Grandma Li takes the children close to their mother. Min hugs them, tears streaming down her face. She hasn't held her girls close for a long time. It is a bit difficult for her to tell who is who. She starts speaking to them, but they remain quiet, their eyes wide and unsure.

Min notices they have lost weight. Grandma Li instructs the girls to give their mother the cherries. Min takes the boxes, her hands trembling, and takes out the cherries, offering them to her daughters.

"Here, eat," she says softly, her voice breaking.

The girls take the cherries, their little hands moving slowly, and begin to eat. Their eyes light up with the sweet taste, and they smile for the first time.

Min watches them, tears blurring her vision. "I missed you so much," she whispers.

Fang, Ling, and Qing, still chewing, reach out and feed their mother cherries with their small hands. Min closes her eyes, savoring the moment, the taste, and the love.

Grandma Li wants the family to be on their own and turns to go to the next room. Ling sees her going away and starts to cry.

Min quickly reassures her. "Grandma isn't going anywhere, my love," she says, hugging her tightly.

For the children, they feel more secure with Grandma Li now that their mother no longer stays with them.

As their visit comes to an end, the girls hug their mother tightly. "We love you, Mommy," they whisper.

"I love you too, my darlings. Be good and listen to Grandma Li," Min replies, her voice breaking. As they leave, the girls turn back, waving at their mother one last time and are ready to leave for their new home with Grandma Li.

In China there are over 1.5 million people serving time, many of them are women who have no choice but to leave their children behind.

Beat of a Heart

Part 1

At the bustling Sealdah Railway Station of Kolkata, the "City of Joy" according to French author Dominique Lapierre, it is a night like any other. At 11 p.m., despite the late hour, the platforms are abuzz with people.

A goods train from the northern state of Uttar Pradesh, running late by eight hours, pulls into Platform No. 10. For RPO Anand, who had already concluded his shift an hour earlier, the train's delayed arrival is frustrating.

"When will we, as Indians, learn to be punctual?" he ponders aloud, knowing well that Hari, the Senior Inspector, and his men will have to return at the crack of dawn to unload the goods.

With a sigh, Anand proceeds with his duty; he cannot shrug off the task of inspecting the cargo though it is well past his scheduled work hours. As he advances along the dimly lit platform, his watchful eye, seasoned by years of service, fixes upon the final compartment. Its door seems to not have been fastened properly. To ensure the security of the goods throughout the night, Anand ascends the metal steps. He undoes the latch and peers into the dark chamber. When he shines his flashlight, what meets his eyes are rows upon rows of rice sacks stacked high. In a corner, the sacks have been rearranged to create a cubicle.

He halts abruptly, his breath heavy. His flashlight has caught in its shine a tiny human hand. Anand's heart skips a beat, but soon his instincts kick in as he swiftly removes the adjacent sacks, revealing a baby. He kneels down, his hands trembling. The tiny baby is so still that a dreadful thought claws at his heart. Memories of his own past losses resurface, emotions choking him as he remembers the day years ago when he had held his own lifeless firstborn.

Transfixed by this fragile life before him, Anand checks for signs of life and, with relief, notes the gentle rise and fall of the baby's chest, the reassuring rhythm of breath. He heaves a sigh of relief. In his mind, he grapples with the idea of someone being so callous-hearted as to leave a baby in a goods train.

The baby lies motionless in his arms. This day, Anand vows, it will be different. This day, he will be a savior, not a helpless father. His soul will not bear the weight of another life lost.

Cradling the baby in one arm, Anand retrieves his phone from the pocket and dials the local Railway Protection Force's emergency number 100 with trembling fingers. Each digit takes an eternity to input. When a voice finally answers on the other end, Anand struggles to find his words. "H-Hello? This-this is the RPO from Sea-Sealdah Station," he stammers, his voice shaking. "I'm, uh, I'm on a goods train, and... I've found a baby. Please…please send help immediately."

There is a moment of silence on the other end, then a surprised voice responds, "A baby in a goods train? Are you sure?"

Yes, yes! I'm holding the baby right now. It's... it's unbelievable. Someone left a baby here. We need help urgently."

The voice on the phone quickly shifts into professional mode. They assure Anand that help is on the way, requesting his location and relevant details about the situation.

Once he ends the call, Anand carefully repositions the fragile baby in his arms. He descends from the train slowly, ensuring the infant is safe with every step. His heart pounds as he makes his way to the nearest bench.

Anand gently sits down, still holding the baby close. The child's quiet breathing provides him some reassurance that he had acted in time. His mind races with questions about the heartless individual who could abandon a helpless infant on a goods train. He looks down at the baby, their eyes meeting, and he whispers soothingly, "You're safe now, little one. Help is coming. You're going to be okay."

Minutes feel like hours as he waits for the Railway Protection Force (RPF) personnel to arrive. The platform is devoid of people now. At last, the distant sound of footsteps breaches the silence. Anand lets out a long breath as he sees women constables dressed in RPF uniforms heading his way. Relief washes over him as he waves them down. The baby lies motionless in his arms.

The RPF officers hurry over, their expressions quickly shifting from curiosity to concern as they see the tiny, pale, motionless baby in Anand's arms. They immediately take charge, inspecting the baby's condition and arranging for medical attention. Childline office-bearers are also informed.Anand provides all the information he can, describing the circumstances in which he found the infant as well as the train's origin.

"We'll need to take the baby to the nearest hospital immediately. We'll also initiate an investigation to determine how this child ended up in such a situation," the RPF officer in-charge states.

Anand nods, his gaze fixed on the baby. Reluctantly, he hands over the tiny bundle to the officer. "Please, can I come along?" he implores.

"Sure," the officer replies, nodding. "After all, you found her."

The nearest hospital is only a kilometer away. Dr. Sen, the chief physician, has been alerted on the urgency of the situation. He carefully assesses the baby's condition.

Anand can't contain his concern. "Is the baby okay?" he asks in a worried voice. He cannot believe the newborn has managed to survive alone for over 36 hours without food.

"Yes," the doctor says after a while. "We'll do everything we can so she can live. We'll run some tests and monitor the baby closely. It is a miracle she is still breathing, but not entirely surprising. Newborns retain some hydration from the amniotic fluid in their system and do not require large amounts of breast milk or formula for the first few days of life. Those fluid reserves help them survive."

Anand nods, still amazed by the baby's resilience.

As the medical professionals continue their efforts, the Childline bearers arrive at the hospital. They comprehend the seriousness of the situation and promptly assume control. With the baby now in safe hands, the RPO officers depart.

Anand lingers, his eyes fixed on the tiny figure swaddled in blankets. He feels an unexpected surge of attachment to the baby he had happened upon by pure accident. The thought of leaving the child alone in the hands of strangers tugs at his heartstrings. Before he could contemplate further, his phone rings. He glances at the screen, his wife's name flashing across it. He realizes suddenly it is past midnight and his family must be worried.

He takes one last look at the baby, who is now being cared for by the Childline bearers. "You're safe now, little one," he whispers, his voice filled with both relief and sadness. "I hope you find a family who loves you."

With a heavy heart, Anand turns and walks out of the hospital. As he steps into the cool night air and heads home, his mind lingers on the fragile life he helped save, grateful for the chance to be a protector.

Part 2

The silence of Sishu Bhavan's nights is often disturbed by the constant cries of a newborn. Savita, an experienced caregiver who has been at the facility for five years, knows these sleepless nights too well. The tiniest babies are also the most sensitive, somehow attuned to touch and scent. Tonight, the infant in her arms proves particularly stubborn, refusing milk despite obvious hunger. Ever since arriving the previous night, she has consistently turned away from the bottle.

Manisha, affectionately known as 'Didi', cradles the baby and offers the bottle again. The baby's cries continue, leaving Savita unsettled. "What now?" she asks, her tone filled with concern.

Didi sighs. "She's probably been breastfed; that's why she won't take the bottle. Where was she found?" "I was just about to tell you, didi," Savita responds promptly. "She was found abandoned in a goods train."

"In a goods train?" Manisha exclaims. "Poor girl, yet she is so beautiful."

"Let's name her 'Chandrima', meaning 'moon-faced'. It suits her perfectly."

Two years later

It is a Sunday morning when a couple walks in, their expressions filled with both hope and nervousness. Mr. and Mrs. Sharma have been longing to adopt a child for years, and today, they visit with the hope of finding their little one.

Savita greets them with a smile. "Welcome to Sishu Bhavan. Chandrima is ready to meet you today."

As they walk through the facility, Mrs. Sharma's eyes catch sight of Chandrima. Her face softens immediately. "Oh, look at her, Raj," she whispers, nudging her husband. "Isn't she just adorable?" Mrs. Sharma kneels down beside Chandrima, her eyes full of warmth. "Hello, Chandrima," she coos softly. "Aren't you just the sweetest thing?"

Chandrima looks at them with wide, curious eyes but remains silent. Mrs. Sharma gently tries to encourage her to speak. "Can you say something, darling? Can you say 'hello'?"

Savita, noticing the interaction, steps in gently. "Chandrima cannot speak yet."

Mr. Sharma straightens up, his expression shifting slightly. "She doesn't talk at all?"

Savita shakes her head. "Not yet, but with time and love, many children find their voice."

Mrs. Sharma's smile fades, concern etching her features instead. "Raj, what do you think?" she asks her husband quietly.

"I don't know, Meera," he replies, his voice hesitant. "We've always wanted a child who can communicate with us. It's going to be difficult if she's non-verbal."

They exchange a look of disappointment, and Mrs. Sharma stands up, brushing her fingers lightly across Chandrima's cheek. "She's so beautiful," she murmurs, "but I don't think we're prepared for this."

Savita watches them with a heavy heart, understanding their concerns but feeling protective of Chandrima. "I understand," she says gently. "It's a big decision."

The Sharmas nod, giving Chandrima one last, lingering look before turning to leave. "Thank you for showing us around," Mr. Sharma says. "We'll think about it and let you know."

As they walk away, Savita lifts Chandrima into her arms, hugging her close. "Don't worry, little one," she whispers. "Your family will find you soon."

Sishu Bhavan, a nurturing home for children up to the age of six, also serves as an adoption center. Two years have passed since Chandrima's name was placed on the adoption list. She has been displaying signs of delayed development. Nearly 20 prospective Indian couples had been drawn to her charm but hesitated due to her lack of speech. Then, a glimmer of hope emerged when Chandrima's file was made available for international adoption. One day, word reached the authorities at Sishu Bhavan that a young couple from Australia had chosen to adopt her.

Part 3

In a corner of the main room, Chandrima sits on a mattress, her small frame leaning against the wall. The room is filled with children; a few are the same age as her, while others are much younger, creating a constant hum of noise. In the center of the room, Savita sits in a chair with a group of children gathered around her. She holds her mobile phone, showing them a cartoon, the colourful images and cheerful sounds making the children laugh. Most of the children sit around doing nothing, having nothing to play with. Five years old now, Chandrima seems content watching the other children, absorbing everything around her. She is oblivious to the fact that in a few days, she will have a completely new life miles away on another continent. In the office next door, arrangements are being made for her to go to Australia, where a loving family and a new home await her.

In Sydney, Oscar and Chloe's home buzzes with excitement as they meticulously pack their bags for a journey they have been waiting for over the past 18 months. Today marks the long-awaited departure for Kolkata, India, where their hearts will finally unite with their beloved daughter, Chandrima. Right at the entrance of their driveway, a cheerful poster proudly declares, 'India Bound: Let's Bring Our Daughter Home!' Oscar's sister drives them to the airport, all three excited.

As Oscar and Chloe touch down at the Kolkata airport seventeen hours later, they are filled with nervous anticipation. This is their first time in India, a land of vivid contrasts and vibrant experiences. Waiting for them is Riya, a representative from 'Sishu Bhawan', who has come to accompany them on their journey to the children's home. As they drive through the streets of Kolkata, their senses are overwhelmed by the vibrant sights, sounds, and smells. They marvel at the colonial-era buildings that seem to burst with old tales. The busy markets are full of colourful produce, vibrant clothing, and the delicious aroma of street food. Street vendors call out their wares, competing with the constant honking of car horns and the ringing of rickshaw bells. Crowds of people move through narrow lanes, haggling over prices, while the scent of spices, fried snacks, and fresh fruits mingles in the air. Shops spill out onto the sidewalks, displaying fabrics, jewellery, and household items, creating a lively and bustling atmosphere unique to Kolkata. It is a symphony of organized chaos, and the couple cannot help but soak in the sights and the sounds of the city.

Finally, Oscar and Chloe stand at the doorstep of Sishu Bhawan, smiling wide, unable to contain their excitement. As they enter, they are welcomed with open arms by Gita, the lady in-charge. "I know you must be so excited," Gita says. "Well, go on. She's upstairs waiting for you."

They climb the steps, each one bringing them a little closer to their cherished dream. Inside the main room, they see children laughing and playing. And then, jumping on a trampoline, there is Chandrima, wearing a bright pink dress. She turns and glances at them with wide, uncertain eyes, but the sight of unfamiliar faces stirs fear, and she bursts into tears. Gita rushes to comfort her. Chloe waves a toy duck, one of the many toys she has brought with her from Sydney, trying to calm her fears, but Chandrima keeps crying. Finally, after an hour or so, when Chloe sits with her on the swing, Chandrima calms down. They start playing on the slide, and Chandrima grows more comfortable at last, later falling asleep in Chloe's arms.

Chandrima also seems to get along well with Daddy Oscar. Oscar is a kind-hearted man who loves children. It doesn't take much effort on his part to make his daughter feel comfortable. They spend several hours trying to make her feel more and more at ease and safe. The next morning, they take her out with them for the first time. It is an emotional moment for Oscar and Chloe. Riya accompanies them. According to the rules of the adoption agency, a child must be comfortable with her adoptive parents before leaving with them.

Their destination is the iconic Victoria Memorial, a renowned landmark in Kolkata that stands as a symbol of the city's rich history and architectural grandeur. Throughout the journey, Chandrima clings to Chloe as if she knows that she has found a mother's touch that will stay forever in her life.

Afterwards, they go to eat at a restaurant. Since it is their first trip to India, they choose to savour a highly famous Indian delicacy: chicken curry and biryani. Riya decides to order a Subway sandwich, something she has never tried before. How ironic that the Westerners are enjoying Indian food while the Indians are trying Western food!

That night in the hotel room, Chandrima sleeps peacefully tucked comfortably between her parents. Their family is now complete. A few days later, they are in Agra to see the Taj Mahal, and Chandrima is all smiles. They have already gotten used to the glances from people around, seeing an Indian baby with an Australian couple. That night in the hotel room, Chandrima sleeps peacefully, tucked between her parents. Their family is now complete. It's time to take their daughter home.

A few more days later, Oscar stands beaming at the Sydney airport, flashing three passports to the authorities. Their entire family has come together to welcome them home: Oscar and Chloe's parents, and Oscar's sister and her children. They hold a world chart showing the incredible journey Chandrima has made, all the way from India to Australia. They stand at the Arrivals, waiting eagerly to see Chandrima, the new baby of their family, with her parents. They can see Oscar coming down the escalator, wearing a T-shirt sporting an Indian flag. Chloe and Chandrima wear T-shirts with the same design. They wave to their family in unencumbered joy. Soon the reunion is filled with hugs and kisses.

As they all stand behind the large banner of the world map, beaming with joy, everyone's eyes are on Chandrima as she claps with joy. Chandrima has finally found love, a family and a home.

Thank you for joining us on this emotional journey through the lives of abandoned children in *Lost Homes*. Their stories are not just tales on pages but mirrors reflecting the resilience, hope, and strength within all of us.

As we close this chapter, let's remember that we hold the power to make a difference in the lives of these children. Take a moment to visit the websites of organizations dedicated to helping children in need, such as UNICEF, Save the Children, and SOS Children's Villages. Your support, whether through donations, volunteering, or spreading awareness, can bring light and hope to those who need it most.

Together, let's build a brighter future for every child, where love and security are not just dreams but realities.

Save the Children
https://balrakshabharat.org/

CRY
https://www.cry.org/about-cry/

Plan International
https://plan-international.org/

Care International

https://www.care-international.org/

UNICEF

https://www.unicef.org/

Education cannot wait

https://www.educationcannotwait.org/

Educate a Child

https://www.unicef.org/partnerships/educate-a-child

War Child

https://www.warchild.net/

www.ingramcontent.com/pod-product-compliance
Lightning Source LLC
Chambersburg PA
CBHW021404150726
47989CB00005B/2395